JANE ASHER'S

CALENDAR
OF
CAKES

JANE ASHER'S

CALENDAR
OF
CAKES

CLAREMONT
BOOKS

This edition published 1995 by
Claremont Books, an imprint of
Godfrey Cave Associates
42 Bloomsbury Street
London WC1B 3QJ

A division of Penguin Books Ltd
Registered offices: Harmondsworth, Middlesex, England

First published 1989

Typeset in Bembo by Goodfellow & Egan, Cambridge
Photographs by Chris Crofton
Diagrams by Gillie Newman
Colour reproduction by Anglia Graphics, Bedford
Printed and bound by Butler and Tanner, Frome, Somerset

ISBN 1-85471-771-5
A CIP catalogue record for this book is available from the British Library

CONTENTS

THE CAKES

INTRODUCTION

EVERY MONTH OF EVERY YEAR contains some special occasion to celebrate, and a cake is one of the best ways of marking such occasions. When you make someone a cake you are not only showing that you appreciate them, but you are giving them some of your time and trouble: a cake personally designed and decorated – however simply or 'unprofessionally' – makes a much more thoughtful present than anything you could buy, and is a lovely centrepiece at a party or family get-together.

When I wrote my first cake book eight years ago I honestly never dreamt anyone would buy it – it was enormous fun to do, but a bit of a family joke, and there was no one more surprised than I was to discover just how many people shared my enthusiasm for decorating cakes and who enjoyed trying out some of my ideas. Over the ensuing years I have naturally made a great many more – including those commissioned by charities, friends and organisations – and I thought it might be time to put down some of these new ideas in another book, together with additional ones specially designed while writing it. As you will see, I have included every sign of the Zodiac, a good standby for birthday cakes if you can't think of any other design.

This is a decorating, not a baking book. I am always more interested in the final look than in the cake within and often use packet cake mixes as my base. I have given a couple of very basic recipes but I leave it up to you to make the cakes as tasty as you like – I shall only help you to make them look good.

I do hope you enjoy these cakes, and that some of them will inspire you to ideas of your own. If you have as much fun making them as I did then it will have been worthwhile.

Finally, just a reminder that the cakes are for special occasions only – we all know the effects of sugar on children's teeth and it's very important that these solidly sweet creations are only consumed a few times a year!

ACKNOWLEDGEMENTS

OWING TO VARIOUS OTHER commitments I found myself having to do this book in something of a rush, and without the help of a wonderful team I would never have been able to design, bake and decorate 39 cakes (yes, there were two ghastly mistakes . . .) in the time. I am deeply grateful to my three special helpers:

My mother Margaret Asher who not only cleared up endlessly and provided sandwiches, coffee and good advice to keep us all going, but who took careful notes about what I was doing and what quantities I used etc., to help me write it all up later.

The brilliant and efficient Sandra Yong, who shopped, baked, iced and decorated tirelessly and without whom the book would not have been possible.

The talented and delightful actress Emma Chambers, who originally came to help wash up, but who was such an excellent pupil that she was soon helping with many of the trickiest decorating jobs.

All the other books I have written have been done entirely at home, but this time my publisher had the wonderful idea of my 'borrowing' a kitchen outside, so that I could fill it with cakes, icing sugar and debris and not have to keep clearing it all away every evening. I was lucky enough to be lent a beautiful new kitchen in one of the show houses in the Chelsea Harbour development by the river in London, and I am very grateful to Globe and to P&O for letting me use it.

I must also thank Kenwood and Magimix, who lent me a food mixer and food processor respectively, both of which proved invaluable (see Equipment, page 17).

Many thanks to Chris Crofton and his assistant Charlie Taylor for so patiently photographing cake after cake, to Patricia Walters for so cleverly designing the book and to Mark Lucas for his usual enthusiastic backing. I am very grateful to Tony Snowdon for photographing the cover so elegantly and for his brilliant spur-of-the-moment jewellery design with my cake cutters and bulldog clips.

Roger Houghton and John Beaton of Pelham Books yet again put up with my being behind on deadlines and gave me support and encouragement far beyond the call of duty.

I would like to thank all the people who have written to me over the years, telling me about their cakes and sometimes sending me pictures – they are always inspiring and it's lovely to know there are so many of you who enjoy cake decorating. Do keep writing.

Lastly, I am very lucky to have a family that puts up with the chaos producing a book inevitably brings (not cake for breakfast *again*, Mum?!) and without their love and inspiration I would have no wish to create cakes in any case.

RECIPES

CAKES

I'm sure you have many tried and tested cake recipes, and you can really use any kind you like for almost all the decorations in this book. If it needs to be shaped then probably a madeira is the best. To calculate how much cake mixture you need use this simple calculation. Fill the cake tin with water, measure it and for each 450ml (¾ pint) make a 1 egg mixture.

BASIC MADEIRA CAKE
To fill a 20cm (8in) round cake tin

225g (8oz) butter or margarine
225g (8oz) caster sugar
4 eggs
225g (8oz) self-raising flour
125g (4oz) plain flour

Mix the two flours together. Cream butter or margarine together with sugar until light and fluffy. Add eggs one at a time, beating well into the mixture and adding a spoonful of flour after each egg. Fold remaining flour into mixture. Turn into a greased and lined tin and level the top. Cook for about 1½ hours in an oven pre-heated to 160°C/325°F/Gas Mark 3 until firm to the touch. Leave for 5 – 10 minutes then turn out and cool on a wire rack.

VARIATIONS

Add grated orange or lemon rind, or replace a tablespoonful of the plain flour with cocoa or coffee powder dissolved in a little warm water.

You may prefer to use fruit cake. It will keep well and is obviously very suitable for Christmas or wedding cakes. Make it ahead of time to let it mature a little.

RICH FRUIT CAKE
To fill a 20cm (8in) round cake tin

250g (8oz) plain flour
pinch of salt
½ teaspoon ground cinnamon
1 teaspoon ground nutmeg
1kg (2lb) mixed fruit
125 g (4oz) shredded almonds
175g (6oz) butter
grated rind ½ lemon
175g (6oz) dark brown sugar
1 tablespoon black treacle
6 eggs
2 tablespoons brandy or rum

Line cake tin with non-stick baking parchment. Sift flour with salt and spices into a mixing bowl and divide this mixture into three portions.

Mix one portion with the fruit and almonds and set aside. Beat the butter until soft, add the lemon rind, sugar and black treacle. Continue beating until the mixture is very soft. Add the eggs, one at a time, beating well between each one, then fold in second portion of the flour mixture. Next mix in the fruit and flour, then the remaining flour mixture and lastly the brandy or rum.

Turn the mixture into the prepared tin and smooth the top. Dip your fingers in warm water and moisten the surface very slightly (this prevents the cake crust from getting hard during the long cooking). Put the cake in the centre of the pre-heated oven at 180°C/350°F/Gas Mark 4 and after one hour reduce the temperature to 160°C/325°F/Gas Mark 3 and cover the top with double thick greaseproof paper or baking parchment. Test after 2 hours with a skewer; when done allow to cool in the tin for about 30 minutes, then turn out onto a rack and leave until quite cold.

Wrap in greaseproof paper or foil and store in an airtight container.

ICINGS

Most of the cakes in this book are decorated with fondant icing, which is extremely easy to use and can be rolled out to cover a cake or modelled with the fingers. You can now buy it ready made in most supermarkets and it really is just as good as homemade and saves a lot of trouble. However, it is obviously more economical to make your own, and the following is a good simple recipe:

FONDANT ICING
450g (1lb) icing sugar
1 egg white★
2 tbsp (30ml) liquid glucose

Warm the glucose to make it easier to spoon out. Mix all the ingredients together in a food proces-sor or by hand until the mixture looks like lumps of breadcrumbs. Turn onto the work surface and knead with the fingers, dusting with icing sugar as necessary to stop it being too sticky. Keep wrapped in clingfilm or in a plastic bag.

When a harder icing is required – such as for the champagne bottle or the Valentine chocolate box – I have recommended using gelatine icing. This is easy to make at home, or you can order packets of ready mix by post (see Addresses, page 19)

GELATINE ICING
450g (1lb) icing sugar
12.5g (½ oz) gelatine powder
4 tbsp (60ml) water
2 tsp (10ml) liquid glucose

Put the water in a heatproof bowl and add the gelatine. Leave to soak for two minutes. Place the bowl in a pan with 1cm (½ in) water and heat gently until the gelatine dissolves. Remove from the heat and stir in the liquid glucose. Allow to cool for two minutes. Turn the mixture into a bowl containing the icing sugar and mix in. If the mixture seems wet add a little more icing sugar until it resembles dough. Wrap in clingfilm or keep in a plastic bag.

Of course a more traditional way of icing cakes is to use royal icing. Many of the cakes in the book can be iced in this way, although it can be tricky to get a really smooth surface. It is also used for the piping of decorations and for sticking pieces of models together.

ROYAL ICING
350g (12oz) icing sugar
1 egg white★

Break the egg white up with a fork and add the icing sugar bit by bit, mixing well after each addition. Add enough to make soft consistency for spreading, stiffer for piping.

WATER ICING

Just add a little water to icing sugar, mixing well, until it is smooth and runny.

You may well want to split some of the cakes and fill them with butter icing. Also you can always stick the fondant onto the cake with a thin layer of butter icing to make it a bit tastier.

BUTTER ICING
225g (8oz) icing sugar
100g (4oz) butter
vanilla essence
15 – 30ml (1 – 2 tbsp) warm water or milk

Cream the butter until soft and gradually beat in the icing sugar, adding a few drops of essence and the milk or water

Orange or lemon

Replace the vanilla essence with a little grated orange or lemon rind and a little of the juice, beating well to avoid curdling the mixture.

Coffee

Replace the vanilla essence with 10ml (2 level tsp) instant coffee powder dissolved in some of the heated liquid.

Chocolate

Either replace 15ml (1 tbsp) of the liquid with 25–40g (1 – 1½oz) melted chocolate, or add 15ml (1 level tbsp) cocoa powder dissolved in a little hot water then cooled.

MARZIPAN

You can make your own if you like, but I really don't think it's worth the trouble. On the whole it's best to use the white type without colouring, but occasionally the yellow can be used to good effect (for the Teddies on page 61 for example).

JAM FOR STICKING

You will need to brush the cakes with jam before covering them with marzipan or fondant. The traditional type is sieved apricot jam, but anything without pips will do. (I have even successfully used redcurrant jelly on occasion). If you warm it first it is easier to use, but it's by no means essential.

★As we are currently advised not to eat raw egg, you may prefer to use dried egg white, adding a little water as directed on the packet.

BASIC TECHNIQUES

Covering a cake with fondant icing

Brush the cake with jam to make it sticky. Dust the work surface well with icing sugar then roll out the fondant icing. Measure the length and height of the side of the cake with a piece of string or tape measure, then cut a piece of icing to fit. Stick it to the cake then trim the top if necessary or other sides if square. Gather up the leftover icing and knead and roll again. Tip the cake upside-down onto the icing and trim round the edge. For oddly shaped cakes you may have to measure several pieces with a tape measure before you fit them onto the cake.

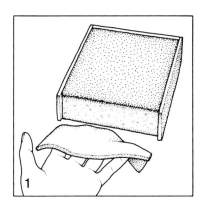 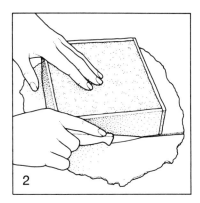

Covering with marzipan

If you are using fruit cakes, you may want to cover them with marzipan first, although even with fruit cake it is not strictly necessary when using fondant, not royal icing. Put the marzipan on in just the same way as for fondant, leaving it a day or so to dry out before icing.

Modelling with fondant

This is just like using plasticine, although you must keep your fingers well dusted with icing sugar, and do always keep the icing wrapped in clingfilm or a plastic bag while you are working, as it will get dry and crusty in the air. Always leave models to dry on non-stick baking parchment.

Colouring fondant

Just knead in drops of food colour bit by bit on the end of a cocktail stick. Wear rubber gloves for the darker colours, or you'll find you walk around looking as if you've just done a murder or cleaned the chimney. I have also discovered while writing this book, that you can knead colour into fondant by using a mixer with the dough hook attached (see Equipment, page 17).

Colouring royal icing

Add drops of food colour bit by bit, starting with tiny bits on a cocktail stick. Mix well into the icing.

Piping

There is no very complicated piping in this book. Most of the designs call for simple lines or blobs piped with a small plain nozzle. Always have a practice on a bit of paper or the back of your hand (except that does tend to mean you eat an awful lot of icing) before you pipe onto the cake, although you'll find you can easily scrape off mistakes with a sharp knife. When you need to pipe a shell pattern just squeeze out the icing in a forwards motion, then draw backwards to leave a wave-like effect.

Polishing the cakes

When you have finished decorating a cake it often has a floury, patchy look from the icing sugar you have used for rolling. If you gently wipe it over with a damp cloth you will find it gives it a lovely smooth finish. You can also use a little cornflour to rub gently over it for extra polish.

Glazing finished decorations

Sometimes a shine can really add the final touch to a cake. Just mix a little glycerine with about half the amount of water and brush it over the icing.

Mistakes

If you're like me, these will be part of your basic techniques! Please don't panic! Almost anything can be scraped off, piled up again or changed into something entirely different (an 'explosion' cake, perhaps?). You can now get an edible white liquid a bit like typewriter corrector fluid, which is very useful for painting out mistakes.

EQUIPMENT

Food colours

You can buy a very good selection of colours from most supermarkets, but for some of the more unusual ones you may need to order by post (see Addresses, page 19). The gold and silver colours, although non-toxic, are not supposed to be eaten, so you must remove any bits of icing decorated with these before eating.

Gold leaf

This is edible but extremely expensive, and so only to be used for very special occasions.

Food processor

I found my Magimix indispensable for mixing icing. It has the great advantage of the lid stopping the sugar flying all over the room. If you make royal icing in it, you can add the colour through the funnel drop by drop with the engine running until you achieve the depth you want.

Food mixer

Up until now I have always coloured fondant by hand, wearing rubber gloves for some of the deeper, more staining colours. Now, however, I have discovered the joy of using my Kenwood mixer with the dough hook attached – it works brilliantly and saves aching arms if you are colouring large quantities. (It is obviously also very useful for mixing cakes!)

Turntable

Can be a great help but is not essential.

Rolling pin and board

A good wooden rolling pin and a large smooth surface for rolling out are essential.

Piping bags

I still prefer to buy the nylon bags, although I know professionals make them from greaseproof paper. There are also now some excellent plastic ones, which although called disposable can be used several times.

Ruler or tape measure

One of these will be needed for many of the cakes.

Non-stick baking parchment

Essential – used in most of the recipes.

Plastic bags or cling film

One or the other will be needed to keep fondant icing in while working.

Paint brushes

An ordinary child's paint brush will usually do, as long as it makes a reasonable point.

Cocktail sticks

These are used in some of the recipes for support or for tracing designs onto cakes.

Flour shaker

Filled with icing sugar, this is very useful for rolling out of fondant.

Rubber gloves

They are very useful when colouring fondant by hand.

Mosaic cutter

Strangely enough I didn't use this for the mosaic (the squares were too big in proportion to the cake) but found it excellent for the crocodile's scales.

ADDRESSES

A LL THE FONDANT I used in the book was bought in packets ready made from the supermarket. Instead of making gelatine icing you can use either Tudor paste or Pastillage which can be ordered in packets to which you just add water. It is very easy to use, quite hard when dry but still edible. I have used it throughout the book.

For Tudor paste, Pastillage or many other ready to mix icings
and all cake decorating equipment and edibles order from the excellent:

Squire's Kitchen,
The Potteries,
Pottery Lane,
Wrecclesham,
Farnham,
Surrey GU10 4QJ
Tel: Farnham (0252) 711749

Equally good for all Sugarcraft supplies (including the colours I
used in this book) you can also order by post from my good friend:

Mary Ford,
Cake Artistry Centre Ltd.,
28, Southbourne Grove,
Bournemouth BH6 3RA
Tel: Bournemouth (0202) 422653 or 431001

The mosaic cutter and the gold leaf can be bought from any good
art shop. Mine came from my favourite:

Green and Stone,
259, Kings Road,
London, SW3
Tel: 01– 352 6521

I bought the heart-shaped cutters and many other bits and pieces from:

Elizabeth David Ltd,
46, Bourne Street,
London, SW1
Tel: 01–730 3123

CAPRICORN

JANUARY *CAPRICORN*

I'VE INTERPRETED CAPRICORN as the Three Billy Goats Gruff (so I suppose it's Capricorn*s*, really). It would be a lovely cake for a children's party – perhaps for a three-year-old, with a candle in each goat?

MEDIUM DIFFICULT.
START TWO DAYS AHEAD.

INGREDIENTS
*1 25cm (10in) cake
1.5 kg (2½lb) fondant
jam for sticking
icing sugar for rolling
350g (¾ lb) white marzipan
225g (½ lb) royal icing
3 or 4 Matchmakers
black, blue, green and
orange food colours*

EQUIPMENT
*30cm (12in) cake board
non-stick baking parchment
cocktail sticks
rubber gloves*

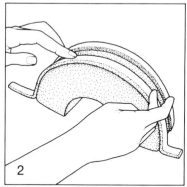

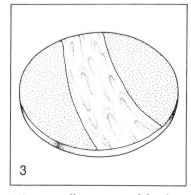

1

Cut the cake in half (perhaps you could freeze the other half, and make a rainbow cake or half-birthday cake out of it later?) Cut a semicircle about 10cm (4in) diameter out of the middle – I used a round tin I happened to have of the right size (fig 1).

Roll two long strips of fondant and stick either side of the top of the 'bridge' to raise the edges to make little walls (fig 2). Allow to dry a little.

Mix a small amount of fondant with blue colouring, only kneading it a little so you achieve a streaky watery effect. Roll and cut out a river about 9cm (3½in) wide and 30cm (12in) long and stick it to the board with a little water. Colour a little more fondant green and stick it either side of the river to be grass (fig 3).

CAPRICORN

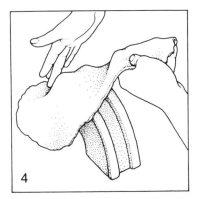

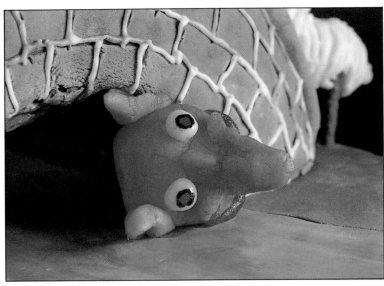

Colour the rest of the fondant grey, by using a little black colour. Jam the cake, roll out the fondant and drape it over (fig 4).

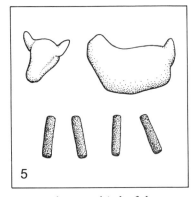

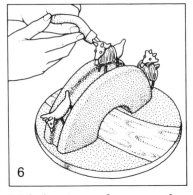

Using about a third of the marzipan model a troll's head. Let dry on baking parchment. With the rest of the marzipan, model three goats of ascending size by making bodies, heads and tails (fig 5).

Stick the pieces of goat together with a little royal icing. Let dry. Break the Matchmakers into suitable sizes for legs and push into the marzipan goats. Position the goats on the bridge, if necessary using cocktail sticks to support them. Pipe the beards, horns, eyes and hair onto the goats (fig 6).

Pipe the 'bricks' onto the bridge. Paint the goats' eyes black and the troll's head as desired. Do remember to remove the cocktail sticks before you eat the cake.

FOOTBALL

FOOTBALL

W HAT A LOVELY SIMPLE cake I thought! Wonderful for a boy's birthday or a team celebration. Just make a round cake in my Christmas pudding tin, cut out a few black and white hexagons and stick them on – simple! If only I'd known . . . I got all my shapes ready and, starting at the top, began sticking them to the cake. All was well for the first couple of rounds but as I worked my way down they just didn't fit; the sphere seemed to get wider. I tried cutting larger shapes – no good. I got a real football and looked at it – ah ha! the white shapes are hexagons but the black shapes are *pentagons*. Still no good. By this time I was going crazy, and decided I needed expert advice. It took maths teacher Miss Pattenden 40 minutes with pencil and paper to explain the trigonometry involved in working out the correct sizes for the shapes.

Now that we've worked out the formula it won't be too difficult for you to calculate your shapes, or you can always make a brightly coloured beach ball instead!

EASY, ONCE YOU KNOW THE CORRECT SIZES!
START DAY BEFORE.

INGREDIENTS
cake cooked in Christmas pudding tin,
or shaped pudding basin cake
450g (1lb) marzipan
jam for sticking
icing sugar for rolling
575g (1¼lb) fondant
black food colouring

EQUIPMENT
cake board
ruler and protractor
cardboard to make templates, or you might be lucky
enough to find patchwork quilt templates of the
right size
rubber gloves

FORMULA FOR MAKING SHAPES:
the internal angles of the hexagons are always 120°.
the internal angles of the pentagons are always 108°
the length of the sides of the shapes is 0.416×the
radius

For example: Our cake was 6cm radius, so we
multiplied that by 0.416 which made 2.496
which we rounded off to 2.5.
So we cut shapes as follows: 12 pentagons with
sides 2.5cm long and internal angles of 108°
20 hexagons with sides 2.5cm long and internal
angles of 120°

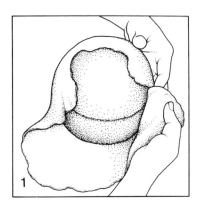

Stick the two halves of the sphere together with jam. Jam the cake and cover with marzipan, trimming as necessary to keep it spherical (fig 1).

Stand the cake with the joins of marzipan tucked underneath. Colour half the fondant black wearing rubber gloves. Roll out the fondant and cut 20 white hexagons and 12 black pentagons and stick them to the cake with a little water (fig 2).

CORNFLAKES

CORNFLAKES

WHAT A VERY SILLY cake! It would be great fun to have several of them on the table – perhaps at a pyjama party so that it looked like breakfast? I've made the bowl out of icing – very easy – but of course you could use a real bowl if you were in a hurry.

EASY. START COUPLE OF DAYS BEFORE IF MAKING AN ICING PLATE, OR SAME DAY WITH REAL BOWL.

INGREDIENTS
225g (½lb) gelatine icing
small round piece of cake, about 12cm (4in) across,
or use scraps or something like a trifle sponge
icing sugar for rolling
jam for sticking
225g (½lb) fondant
orange food colour
225g (½lb) water icing
sugar

EQUIPMENT
china bowl about 18cm (7in) across

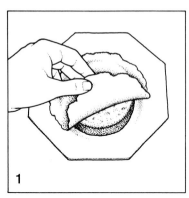

Mould an icing bowl (just as for Spaghetti plate, page 69). When the bowl is dry and hard, put the piece (or scraps) of cake into it. Spread the cake with jam. Roll out half the fondant and cover the cake (fig 1). Press against the sides of the bowl – very gently – so there are no gaps.

Colour the remaining fondant cornflake colour and tear little scraps off and press them upright onto the fondant, damping with a little water to make them stick (fig 2).

Mix up the water icing and add a fraction of orange colour to make it creamy looking. Pour over the cornflakes (fig 3).

Sprinkle with a little sugar (as if it isn't sweet enough already!)

AQUARIUS

THIS CAKE WOULD MAKE a magnificent centrepiece at a formal celebration. The effect of the mosaic icing tiles is really quite spectacular, but it does take quite a bit of patience.

MEDIUM DIFFICULTY.
START SEVERAL DAYS AHEAD, DEPENDING ON DESIGN.

INGREDIENTS
225cm (10in)×35cm (14in) cakes
1.5kg (3lb) fondant
jam for sticking
icing sugar
1.25kg (2½lb) of fondant for tiles
450g (1lb) royal icing
assorted food colours as required by design and
including black

EQUIPMENT
tomato slicer
37cm (15in)×52cm (21in) piece of
hardboard cut to size
piping bag with small nozzle
tracing paper and pencil
rubber gloves

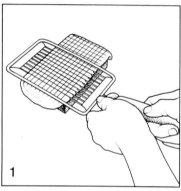

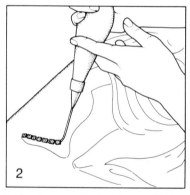

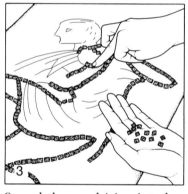

Jam the cakes and cover with the fondant. Let dry for a few hours. Push the two cakes together on the board and stick with a little royal icing. Trace a design onto the cakes (see page 49). Wearing rubber gloves, colour a small amount of fondant black. Roll it out and drape over a small packet or similar to raise it up for cutting (the tomato slicer is tricky to use on the flat). Dust the slicer well with icing sugar and press into the icing. Don't cut right through or it's impossible to extricate the icing from the slicer. Turn the icing and mark across the other way to make squares (fig 1).

Lift the marked icing off the packet and let it dry a little while you continue mixing and marking other colours. When the icing has dried a little you'll find it's easy to break into neat squares. (Using the tomato slicer was my mother's brilliant invention, but you may well find something else equally good.) Pipe sections of the outline on the cake with a small plain nozzle and royal icing, then stick black tiles onto the icing. I found it easiest to do the outline first (fig 2).

Spread the royal icing into larger areas with a knife or back of a teaspoon, then stick tiles (fig 3). If all the family took turns, or you gathered a group of friends to help, you'd be surprised how quickly the surface would get covered.

When all the cake is covered (hooray!) clean the tiles with a damp brush to remove any surplus icing and bring out the colours. You could shine them with glycerine but I think they look more realistic matt.

VALENTINE'S DAY

VALENTINE'S DAY

WHAT COULD BE MORE romantic than a heart-shaped box of chocolates topped with a red rose? (Well, a few diamonds perhaps . . .) The whole of this cake is edible; even the 'chocolates' are made out of cake and the 'paper cases' of chocolate. You could always fill it with real chocolates instead (or real diamonds?)

MEDIUM DIFFICULTY.
START 3 OR 4 DAYS AHEAD.

INGREDIENTS
1 cake cooked in a heart-shaped tin
jam for sticking
icing sugar for rolling
675g (1½lb) gelatine icing
350g (¾lb) plain chocolate cake covering
350g (¾lb) fondant
pink, green and red food colours
glycerine water for glazing

EQUIPMENT
heart-shaped cake tin
cake board
paint brush
non-stick baking parchment

For the chocolates
INGREDIENTS
1 cake cooked in a 25cm×20cm (10in×8in) tin
350g (¾lb) plain chocolate cake covering
125g (¼lb) milk chocolate cake covering
125g (¼lb) white chocolate
assorted toppings for chocolates

EQUIPMENT
tiny cutters
paper or preferably foil petits fours cases
cocktail sticks
cake rack

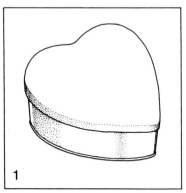

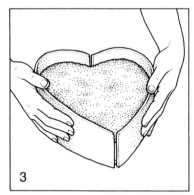

Colour the gelatine icing pink. Dust outside of cake tin with icing sugar. Roll out half the gelatine icing and drape it over the bottom of the tin. Trim it to form a neat lid (fig 1). Knead leftover icing back into the other half you have kept back. Leave lid to dry for two days, then ease it carefully off the tin.

Measure the sides and height of the cake. Roll and cut two strips about 4cm (1½in) higher than the cake sides. Prop them inside the dusted cake tin to support them (fig 2).

Leave the sides in the tin for a few minutes until they are dry enough not to flop over but still bendable. Jam the sides of the cake and stick the icing on (fig 3).

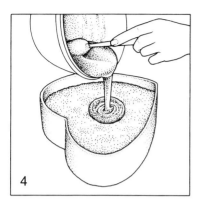

4

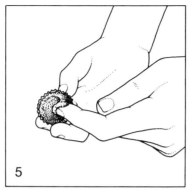

5

6

Join the sides with little strips of wetted icing at top and bottom of the heart shape so there are no gaps. Melt the plain chocolate over hot water or in a microwave. Pour it carefully into the top of the cake (fig 4). Leave to set.

Using melted plain chocolate, coat the inside of the petits fours cases with the finger, adding bit by bit until a good layer is built up (fig 5). Leave to set (in the fridge in hot weather). When completely hard carefully peel away the cases.

Cut little shapes out of the extra cake (fig 6). Push a cocktail stick into each one and dip and swirl in melted white, plain or milk chocolate. Ease it off the cocktail stick by using another stick to push it gently onto the cake rack, with a tray underneath to catch the surplus. When still slightly sticky, press decoration into the top.

When set, place the little 'chocolates' in their cases and arrange in the box. Colour about two-thirds of the fondant red, and a tiny amount green and make a large rose and two leaves as for Rose Bowl (page 79). Measure diagonally across the top of the box. Colour the remaining fondant dark pink and measure and cut a ribbon to fit. Stick the ribbon to the box lid with a little water. Cut two short lengths of ribbon and shape the ends. Stick to centre of lid, then add the rose and leaves. Glaze the ribbon and rose if desired with the glycerine water.

TOM KITTEN

TOM KITTEN

THIS IS THE ONLY CAKE that has ever been exhibited at the Tate Gallery in London! I was reading some stories to children as part of the wonderful Beatrix Potter exhibition they held there and they asked me to make a cake to display at the same time. The story of how poor Tom Kitten was wrapped in suet pastry by the wicked Samuel Whiskers and his wife had made a deep impression on me as a child, so I decided to use that as my theme.

EASY.
START TWO DAYS BEFORE TO LET HEAD DRY.

INGREDIENTS
1 large bought swiss roll
jam for sticking
icing sugar for rolling
450g (1lb) white marzipan
450g (1lb) fondant
blue, black and brown food colours

EQUIPMENT
A copy of The Tale of Samuel Whiskers by Beatrix Potter
non-stick baking parchment
kitchen paper
paint brush

TOM KITTEN

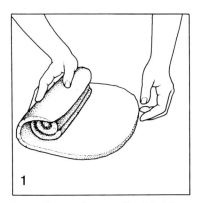

1

Dust the surface well with icing sugar. Roll out the marzipan quite thickly. Jam the cake and roll it up in the marzipan, tucking the ends in neatly (fig 1).

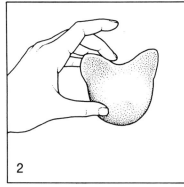

2

Mould a head out of half the fondant, using a picture of Tom Kitten from the book as a guide (fig 2).

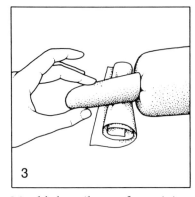

3

Mould the tail out of remaining fondant. Stick it to one end of the cake and prop it with kitchen paper (fig 3).

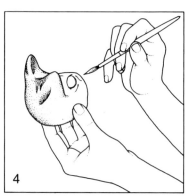

4

Paint the head and tail with food colours, again looking at the book to copy (fig 4). When the head is dry stick in position.

MARCH *PISCES*

PISCES

I HAD ALL SORTS OF ambitious plans to put toffee glass over the sides of this so that it looked like a real tank, but it proved impossible. It was so thick and swirly that you couldn't see the fish at all, which rather defeated the purpose of the whole thing.

EASY WITHOUT FRAME, START AT LEAST TWO DAYS AHEAD IF YOU WANT TO INCLUDE IT – IT CAN BE VERY FIDDLY.

INGREDIENTS
2 26cm (10 ½in)×13cm (5in) cakes
1kg (2¼ lb) fondant
350g (¾lb) gelatine icing
jam for sticking
icing sugar for rolling
125g (¼lb) royal icing
blue, green, orange and silver food colours

EQUIPMENT
cake board
non-stick baking parchment
paint brush
piping bag with small nozzle

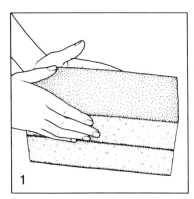

1

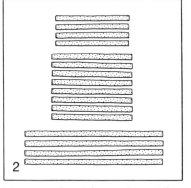

2

Stick the cakes one on top of the other with jam (or use butter icing if you like) (fig 1). Stand it up on its long side.

Measure the sides and uprights of the cake. Roll out the gelatine icing and cut 8 strips 2cm (1in) higher than the cake, 4 to the width of the cake, and 4 to the length of the cake (fig 2). Let dry on baking parchment for a couple of days.

Keep back a little fondant to make fish, etc. Colour the rest bluey-green. Jam the cake and cover sides and top with rolled out pieces of fondant. Cut fish, weeds, stones out of coloured fondant and stick to tank with a little water or jam. Stick dry tank pieces to cake and to each other with royal icing. When dry paint silver.

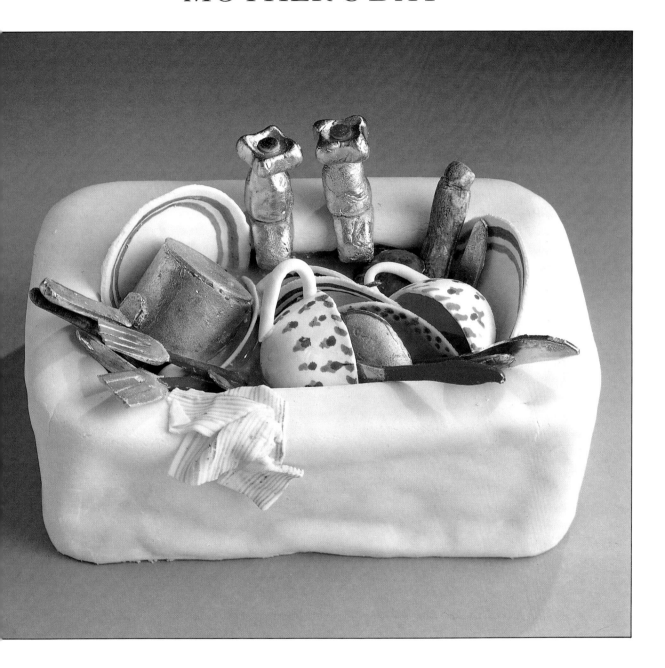

MOTHER'S DAY

I THINK A LOT OF MUMS would appreciate the joke of being given a sink full of dirty washing-up for their cake – especially if you make sure they don't have to do any *real* washing-up on their special day. If it's a bit too depressingly like real life then you could always make the bowl of roses instead (page 79).

MEDIUM DIFFICULTY.
START COUPLE OF DAYS BEFORE TO LET CROCKERY DRY.

INGREDIENTS
1 cake 23cm×17cm×8cm (9in×6½in×3in)
jam for sticking
icing sugar for rolling
125g (¼lb) gelatine icing
675g (1½lb) fondant
assorted food colours, including silver
225g (½lb) water icing

EQUIPMENT
dolls' tea-set for moulding
paint brush
non-stick baking parchment

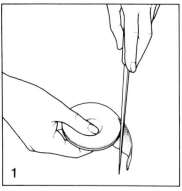

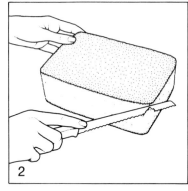

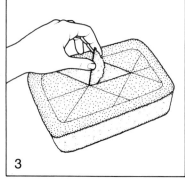

Dust the dolls' tea-set pieces with icing sugar. Roll out the gelatine icing and drape over the pieces, moulding and trimming to fit (fig 1). Leave to dry. Remove carefully. Model taps and knives, forks etc. Leave to dry on baking parchment.

Trim the cake into a sink shape (fig 2).

Mark the bowl with a knife, then score sections and pull them out with the fingers (fig 3).

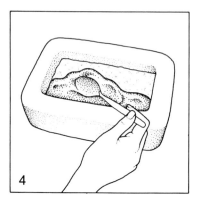

Jam the cake. Roll out the fondant and drape it over, slashing it so it can fall into the bowl. Line inside of bowl with another piece of fondant (to prevent water icing seeping away) (fig 4).

Paint the taps silver and stick them onto the back of the sink. Paint the crockery and cutlery and when dry position in the bowl. Colour the water icing pale blue and pour it into the sink. Leave to set.

CHAMPAGNE BOTTLE

CHAMPAGNE BOTTLE

T HIS IS REALLY MORE of a surprise centrepiece than a cake. You can fill it with all sorts of delicious mixtures – from strawberries and cream to chocolates – and just break it open at the right moment.

MEDIUM DIFFICULTY.
START SEVERAL DAYS AHEAD.

INGREDIENTS

For bottle
675g (1½lb) gelatine icing
green food colouring
icing sugar for rolling
225g (½lb) cooking chocolate or
chocolate cake covering

For label and foil
rice paper
red food colouring
black food colouring pen
225g (½lb) fondant
gold leaf or gold food colouring

EQUIPMENT
champagne bottle
felt-tip pen or preferably chinagraph pencil
cake board
Blu-Tack or plasticine
plastic bag

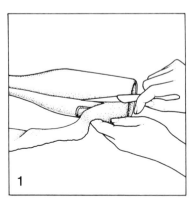

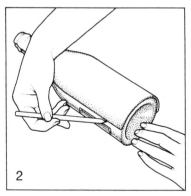

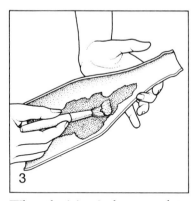

Carefully soak the labels off the champagne bottle and keep as templates. Mix green colouring into the icing until it is a good bottle colour. Dust the real bottle liberally with icing sugar. Roll out half of the gelatine icing and drape it over the bottle, then trim to half-way down the sides (fig 1).

Wedge the bottle with small pieces of Blu-Tack or plasticine so that it doesn't roll. Mark the bottle where the icing finishes with the felt-tip or chinagraph pencil (fig 2).

When the icing is dry enough to move (about 24 hours or less) remove it carefully and make the other half bottle, matching the edges of the icing to the marks on the bottle. Keep left-over scraps in a plastic bag. Let the half bottle dry and remove carefully. Paint the insides of the bottle halves with melted chocolate. This stops the filling making the bottle soggy (fig 3).

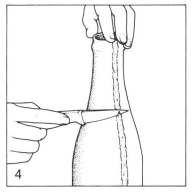

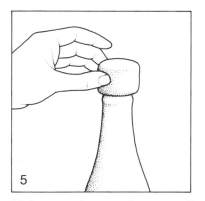

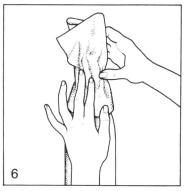

Use dampened strips of the left–over gelatine icing to join the halves together, trimming as necessary (fig 4).

Make a cork out of scraps of icing and press onto the top of the bottle (fig 5). Let dry.

Cut labels out of rice paper and decorate with the food colour-ings. Roll out the 225g (½lb) fondant very thinly and scrunch over the top of the bottle (fig 6).

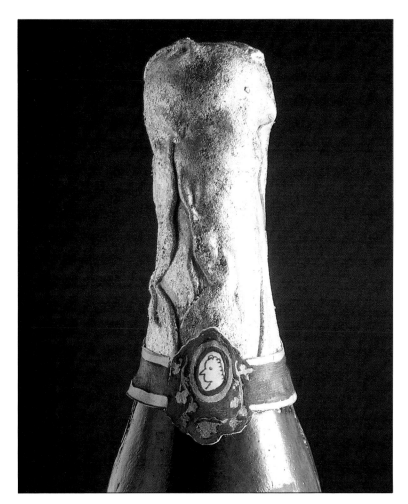

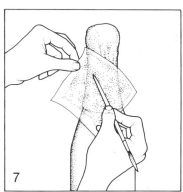

Rub the gold leaf onto the icing. This takes time and you have to be very patient (fig 7). Using real gold leaf is very extravagant but for a really special occasion it's worth it. It looks magnifi-cent and is edible. Alternatively paint it with gold colouring, but remember to remove it before eating.

Stick the labels onto the bottle with a little fondant mixed with water. Fill as desired from the bottom.

ARIES

APRIL *ARIES*

THIS COMBINATION OF CUT OUT fondant and piped butter icing gives the Ram a good fleecy look. You could use it for all sorts of other ideas: anything where you wanted a raised, furry texture.

EASY.
START ONE DAY AHEAD.

INGREDIENTS
1 30cm (12in)×23cm (9in) cake (I used my roasting tin)
675g (1½lb) fondant to cover cake
jam for sticking
icing sugar for rolling
125g (¼lb) fondant for ram
250g (½lb) butter icing
black, yellow and green food colours

EQUIPMENT
black food colouring pen
piping bag with large star nozzle
paper and pencil
cake board

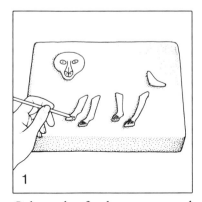

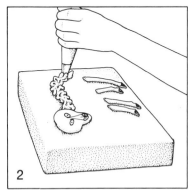

Colour the fondant green and cover the cake with it. Draw (or trace from a magazine and enlarge) a ram on a piece of paper and cut it out. Cut the legs, head and tail off so they are separate. Roll out the white fondant and cut out legs, head and tail, using your pieces of paper as templates. Save the scraps of icing to make horns. Position the pieces of fondant on the cake, using the paper body to give you an idea where they should go. Add black hooves and features with the food pen (or a brush and black colouring) (fig 1).

Colour the butter icing very pale yellow and put into the piping bag. Pipe the wool, making swirly, shaggy patterns (fig 2).

Colour leftover scraps of fondant black, shape into curly horns and stick to ram's head with a little water. Prop with crumpled kitchen paper so they dry upright (fig 3).

EASTER

APRIL

EASTER

I ORIGINALLY MADE THIS CAKE for the third anniversary of the Terry Wogan show. I'd already made him two cakes on previous occasions so I was looking for a new idea. 'What do you think of if I say "Wogan"?' I asked my husband. 'Rabbit, rabbit, rabbit . . .' he replied. So there it was. You obviously needn't make a number if it's for Easter, they would look lovely clustered round any shape of cake.

MEDIUM DIFFICULTY.
START FEW DAYS AHEAD TO GIVE TIME TO MAKE RABBITS.

INGREDIENTS
cake cooked in a large 3 shape
jam for sticking
icing sugar for rolling
675g (1½lb) fondant
450g (1lb) royal icing
pink food colour
1.8kg (4lb) fondant to make rabbits

EQUIPMENT
large round cake board
piping bag with shell and No 2 nozzles
non-stick baking parchment

EASTER

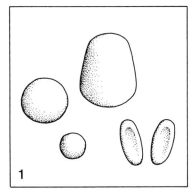

Model about 34 rabbits (!) from the fondant (fig 1). Let them dry on the baking parchment.

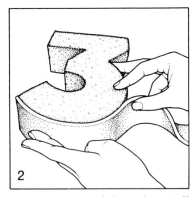

Jam the sides of the cake. Roll out about two-thirds of the fondant and cut strips to cover the sides (fig 2).

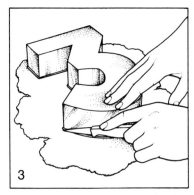

Cover the top of the cake by turning it upside down onto the rolled out icing, or by using the cake tin as a template (fig 3).

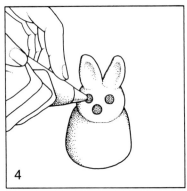

Colour the royal icing pink. Pipe shell pattern round the top of the cake. Pipe features onto the rabbits (fig 4) and then paint the insides of ears pink. Position rabbits round cake.

FIRST FOLIO

FIRST FOLIO

I FIRST MADE THIS last year for the inauguration of the rebuilding of Shakespeare's Globe theatre on the South Bank. It was Shakespeare's birthday (April 23rd) and Dame Judi Dench dug the first hole with a huge JCB and then fireworks and water cannons were let off. It was all very exciting and I think Will would have been very proud.

It's unlikely you will want to celebrate such a relatively obscure anniversary but I thought it would show you how effective a book can look if you trace a fairly intricate design onto it. This is a very large cake, but you could easily scale it down.

MEDIUM DIFFICULTY.
START SEVERAL DAYS AHEAD, DEPENDING ON THE DESIGN YOU CHOOSE.

INGREDIENTS
2 large rectangular sponge cakes
(mine were 25cm×20cm (10in×8in)
jam for sticking
icing sugar for rolling
1.8kg (4lb) gelatine icing
(you can use ordinary fondant, but the gelatine icing
dries harder and so is easier to draw on)
red and gold food colours or gold leaf

EQUIPMENT
picture for tracing
tracing paper
(I used baking parchment, as I had some anyway)
pencil
food colouring pen
large cake board or piece of hardboard
paint brush

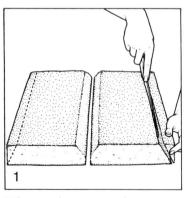

1

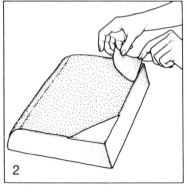

2

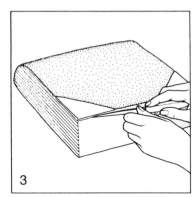

3

(These cakes are so large, you may want to split them and fill with butter icing first.) Trim both cakes into a book shape (fig. 1).

Work on one cake at a time. Roll out a small amount of the icing, jam the corners of the cake then cover with icing (fig 2).

Cover the sides of the cake with icing, then mark pages quickly by drawing a knife along (fig 3).

4

Cover the top and pull back the corners to look like curled pages (fig 4).

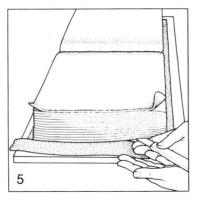

5

Cover the other cake similarly. Place the cakes together on the board. You should have used about three-quarters of the icing. Colour the remainder red, then cut strips to go round the cake to look like the cover. Tuck them under the edges of the cake, keeping leftovers to make the marker (fig 5). Let the icing dry for a day or so.

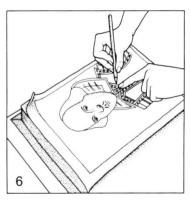

6

Trace the drawing onto the paper. Turn the drawing over and rub the pencil over the lines you have drawn. Position the paper on the cake, then draw over the original lines again, so that the picture is transferred onto the cake – don't worry, pencils nowadays are non-toxic! (fig 6).

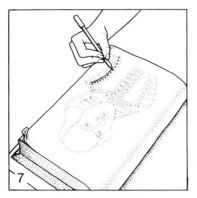

7

With the food colouring pen, carefully draw over the pencil marks on the cake (fig 7).

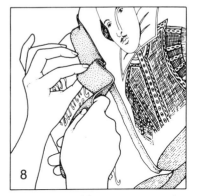

8

Write a suitable message on the opposite page. Fill any gap in the middle of the book with icing, then roll out a marker and drape onto the centre (fig 8).

Paint the pages with gold colouring or rub with gold leaf, removing them before eating if you use the colour.

TAURUS

MAY *TAURUS*

THIS TECHNIQUE IS CALLED making a run-out, and can be used in many different ways. You can even trace a pattern onto baking parchment and make the run-out on the paper. It has to be left to dry for some time (a few days) and then carefully removed. It can be very useful, especially if you make something like an ice-cream cake which you want to decorate at the last minute, but this way of doing it directly onto the cake is much easier.

MEDIUM DIFFICULT.
START FEW DAYS AHEAD.

INGREDIENTS
1 25cm (10in) round cake
675g (1½lb) plain chocolate cake covering
225g (½lb) royal icing
brown food colouring

EQUIPMENT
paper and pencil
piping bag with shell, No 2 and 3 nozzles
paint brush
cocktail stick
wire rack

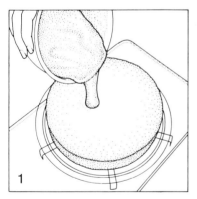

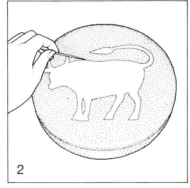

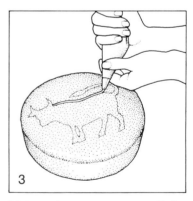

Stand the cake on a wire rack with a dish or tray underneath. Melt half the cake covering over hot water or in a microwave and pour it over the cake, scooping up the surplus from the tray and spreading it onto the side of the cake if necessary (fig 1). Leave to harden.

Draw a bull on the paper and cut it out. Put the bull on the cake and gently scratch round the shape with the cocktail stick (fig 2).

Using about a quarter of the royal icing, fill a piping bag with No 2 nozzle and carefully pipe round the scratched outline (fig 3). Let dry for an hour or so.

TAURUS

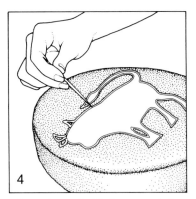

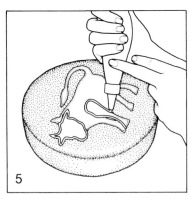

Thin about half the remaining icing with water or egg white. Fill the piping bag with No 3 nozzle and flood the bull shape with the runny icing, using the cocktail stick to ease it into every corner (fig 4).

Let dry for a few hours. Use stiff royal icing to overpipe the details of head and legs onto the bull (fig 5).

Flood the details in the same way as before. When dry, paint details with brown colour. Melt the remaining chocolate and pipe shell pattern round edges of cake.

FOR TEA

FOR TEA

I FIRST MADE THIS FOR my brother's fortieth birthday (For Tea – Forty . . .) and then I made it again for the fortieth anniversary of Woman's Hour. It didn't strike me until later how extraordinary it was to be spending hours decorating a cake for the radio. They described it beautifully to the listeners, but it did all seem rather silly . . .

DIFFICULT.
START TWO DAYS AHEAD.

INGREDIENTS
2 pudding basin cakes
jam for sticking
450g (1lb) fondant
icing sugar for rolling
450g (1lb) gelatine icing
small quantity of royal icing for sticking
125g (¼lb) water icing
orange, brown, green and silver food colours

EQUIPMENT
real teapot, cup, saucer and spoon for moulding
cake board
piping bag with No 3 nozzle

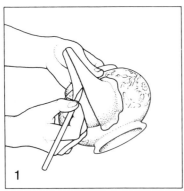

Dust half a real teapot spout with icing sugar then cover with a little rolled out gelatine icing. Mark where the half comes to with a felt-tip or chinagraph pencil (so you will be able to make the other half to fit) (fig 1).

Mould a teacup shape the same way you did the spout. When dry, stick the two halves of the spout and the teacup together (fig 4).

Trim the fondant away to leave a neat half spout (fig 2).

When the half spout is dry make another one the other side. Then mould a handle over the teapot handle and let dry. Mould a lid the same way (fig 3).

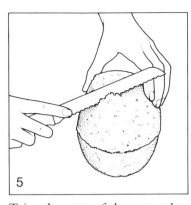

5

Trim the tops of the two cakes and stick them together with jam (or butter icing). Shape them to a more rounded teapot shape. Keep the trimmings for filling the cup (fig 5).

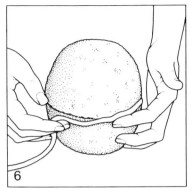

6

With a little of the fondant, fill in any gap at the join (fig 6).

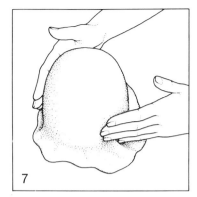

7

Spread the cakes with jam then roll out the remainder of the fondant and drape over the cakes (fig 7).

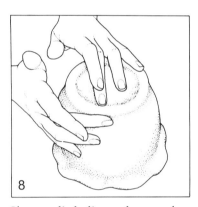

8

Shape a little lip at the top that the lid will fit into, then trim and tuck the extra fondant at the bottom (fig 8).

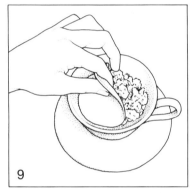

9

Mould a saucer (see Spaghetti, page 69) and a teaspoon. Model a little handle and stick onto the cup. Stick the cup onto the saucer and fill with cake crumbs. Cut a circle from left over fondant and place over the crumbs (fig 9).

10

Paint teaspoon silver. Stick spout and handle onto teapot. Position lid. Colour the water icing tea colour and pour into top of cup (fig 10). Let dry. Paint pot, cup and saucer as desired. Position teaspoon.

CHRISTENING

CHRISTENING

THERE ARE FEW MORE joyful occasions than that of welcoming a new baby into the world and giving him/her a name. There are many religious themes that make wonderful christening cakes, but I thought this jolly chap announcing his arrival would make a change, and is not difficult to do. You could even use a baby doll if you don't want to model one out of icing. With a new baby in the house there certainly won't be much time for fiddling about – if your baby is anything like mine were it's an achievement just to get yourself dressed in the morning . . .

EASY.
START DAY BEFORE.

INGREDIENTS
20cm (8in) round sponge
675g (1½ lb) fondant
icing sugar for rolling
jam for sticking
pink and blue food colours
125g (¼lb) water icing
125g (¼lb) royal icing

EQUIPMENT
cocktail sticks
piping bag with No 2 nozzle
paint brush

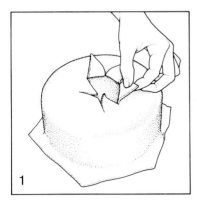

over the cake. Make slashes in the middle and pull back pieces of fondant (fig 1).

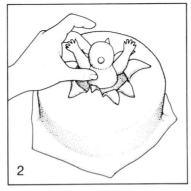

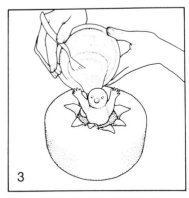

Colour about a quarter of the fondant pink and model the top half of the baby, using the cocktail sticks to support his arms if necessary. Leave to dry a little on baking parchment. Spread jam all over cake *except* for a circle in the middle about 10cm (4in) diameter. Roll out the remaining fondant and drape

Cut a small hole in the middle of the cake. Push the baby into it (fig 2).

Trim the bottom of the cake. Pipe features on the baby and add a sash and name if desired. Pour the water icing into the gap round the baby (fig 3).

Pipe a message with the royal icing on top of the cake and paint the features. Please remember to remove the cocktail sticks before eating the cake.

GEMINI

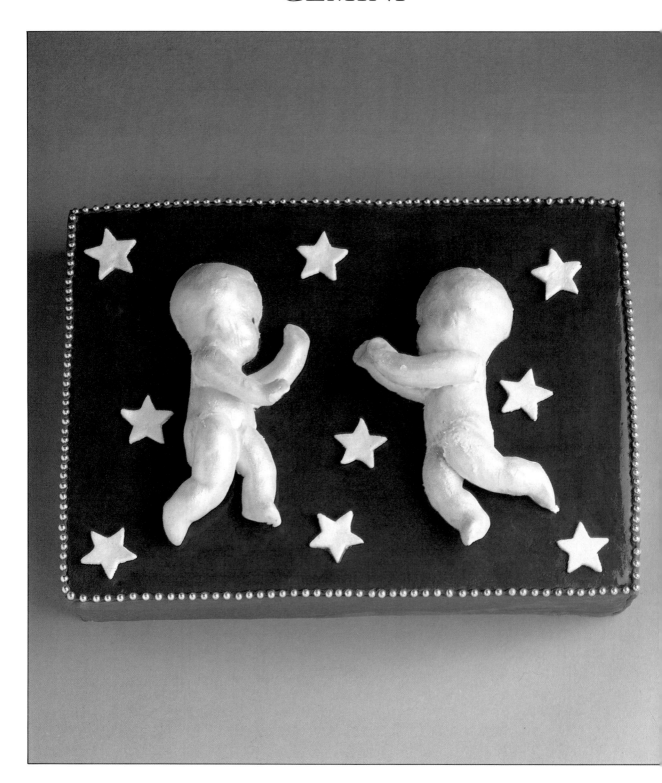

JUNE *GEMINI*

T**HE SIXTH OF OUR** Zodiac signs. Geminis are supposed to be artistic, volatile and with two sides to their nature. I'm married to one, so at least can vouch for the fact that they get on pretty well with Arians . . . The sparkle powder mixed with water gives a lovely pearly unearthly sheen to the twins, but if you can't get hold of it they look fine just plain pink.

MEDIUM DIFFICULTY.
START TWO DAYS AHEAD.

INGREDIENTS
225g (½lb) gelatine icing
1 rectangular cake
(mine is about 33cm×23cm (13in x9in))
jam for sticking
icing sugar for rolling
675g (1½lb) fondant
blue, pink and yellow colourings
pink sparkle colour
125g (¼lb) royal icing
silver balls

EQUIPMENT
real doll to mould from
piping bag and small nozzle
star cutter
cake board
rubber gloves
paint brush

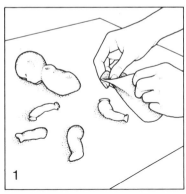

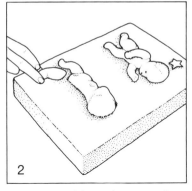

Colour the gelatine icing pale pink. Dismember the doll (!) and dust with icing sugar. Mould half the head and torso, half both arms and legs, all from the same side. When dry, remove the icing shapes carefully. Turn the doll pieces over and do the same on the other sides (fig 1).

Wearing rubber gloves, colour the fondant a deep night-sky blue, keeping back a little to make the stars. Jam the cake then cover with the blue fondant. When the doll pieces are dry, paint the features and hair. Mix the sparkle colour with a little water and paint over the twins, then position on the cake, sticking in position with royal icing (fig 2).

Prop up the upper limbs as necessary with any suitable sized object until they are dry (fig 3).

Cut out stars from the remaining fondant and dust with sparkle. Stick on the cake. Colour the remaining royal icing dark blue, pipe a line round the edge of the cake and stick silver balls all round.

FATHER'S DAY

JUNE

FATHER'S DAY

T HIS TEDDY WAS JUST about to settle down and read his newspaper when he was invaded. He might pretend to mind, but he's actually rather pleased to have his son and daughter clambering all over him – he knows only too soon they'll be far too busy being grown-up and 'cool' to have time for a cuddle. This lovely idea for a cake was given to me by my friend, four-year-old Elizabeth Yong.

MEDIUM DIFFICULTY.
START TWO DAYS BEFORE.

INGREDIENTS
1 15cm (6in) square cake
2 mini rolls
675g (1½lb) fondant
jam for sticking
icing sugar for rolling
675g (1½lb) yellow marzipan
gold balls
brown, pink, blue, orange and black food colours

EQUIPMENT
cake board
non-stick baking parchment
paint brush

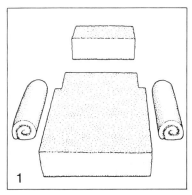

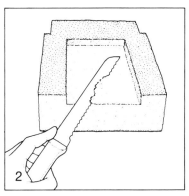

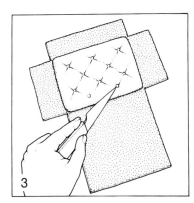

Cut a strip about 3cm (1¼in) off one side of the cake. Shorten the strip by about 4cm (1½in). This will form the back of the chair. Shape the bottom of the chair by cutting little indentations each side at the back (fig 1).

Carve out the seat of the chair (fig 2).

Cover the small piece of cake with marzipan. Mark 'deep buttoning' with a knife. Colour most of the fondant brown, keeping back a little to make clothes. Roll out a small amount of fondant and cut to shape as shown to cover the back of the chair (fig 3). Stick with jam.

FATHER'S DAY

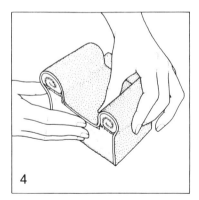

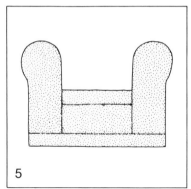

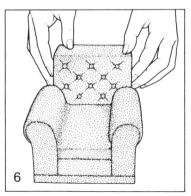

Stick the mini rolls to either side of the chair with jam. Roll and cut a strip of fondant and drape it right over the chair and arms as shown (fig 4).

Roll out more fondant. Without jam, turn the chair front down on top of it and cut round to get the right shape. Lift off the chair, mark the fondant as shown, then stick to front of chair (fig 5). Press gold balls into the seam.

Stick the back of the chair in place with jam (fig 6).

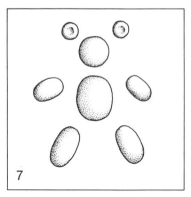

Make teddy bears by moulding pieces as shown (fig 7).

Stick bear pieces together. Add little coloured pieces of fondant for clothes (the skirt is pleated in the same way as the Bride's sleeves (page 99). Paint features.

WEDDING

THIS IS EXTREMELY QUICK and easy to do, unlike most wedding cakes, and would suit a jolly young couple who don't fancy a more traditional cake. I think it looks young and bright and full of fun, and if you're in love and about to be married what could be more suitable?

EASY.
START TWO DAYS BEFORE (OR EARLIER).

INGREDIENTS	EQUIPMENT
3 8cm (3in) deep cakes, 15cm (6in), 20cm (8in) and 25cm (10in) diameter	1 20cm (8in), 1 25cm (10in) and 1 30cm (12in) cake board
jam for sticking	wedding cake pillars
icing sugar for rolling	lolly stick
2kg (4½lb) white marzipan (optional)	3 heart-shaped cutters, measuring from centre of
2.5kg (5½lb) fondant	top to point
about 12 packets of chocolate beans,	4cm (1¾in), 4.5cm (1⅞in) and 7cm (3in)
depending on what colours you want and	piping bag with No 2 nozzle
what are in the packets	non-stick baking parchment
675g (1½lb) royal icing	
red food colour	

Cover the cakes with fondant (or royal icing, with or without marzipan, see p.15). Use about 450g (1lb) for the smallest cake, about 675g (1½lb) for the middle cake and about 900g (2lb) for the large one. Ice the sides first then the top, so the seam is on the side.

Colour the remaining fondant red. For the large cake cut out 8 medium hearts and stick them on with a little royal icing at 10cm (4in) intervals. For the medium cake cut 7 medium hearts and stick on at 9½cm (3¾in) intervals and for the small cake cut 6 small hearts and stick at 9cm (3½in) intervals. Cut two large hearts and let them dry on baking parchment.

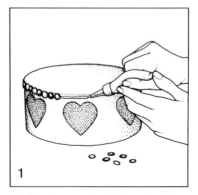

Stick cakes to their boards. Sort chocolate beans into colours, and make sure you have enough before you start. Pipe lines of royal icing round the top and bottom of each cake, and stick chocolate beans as you go before icing dries (fig 1).

Spread one large heart with royal icing then, placing lolly stick in between, cover with other large heart (fig 2). Let dry.

Pipe round edge of large heart and decorate with chocolate beans. Make slot in top of small cake with sharp knife, and gently push lolly stick into it, so the large heart stands up. Let all the icing dry well. Mount cakes on pillars at the last moment, as fondant and madeira cake is not as strong as the traditional fruit cake and royal icing.

JULY *CANCER*

CANCER

AN IRRESISTIBLE SIGN TO make into a cake. The smooth, shiny shell of the crab reproduces beautifully in icing, and the slight marbling effect just finishes it off. I suppose you could always add a huge pink icing foot with its toe being pinched . . .

MEDIUM DIFFICULTY.
START DAY BEFORE.

INGREDIENTS
25cm (10in) round cake
225g (½lb) marzipan
1.1kg (2½lb) fondant
jam for sticking
icing sugar for rolling
orange, red, brown and yellow food colours
scraps of licorice
glycerine water for glazing

EQUIPMENT
cake board
small piece of sponge for marbling
rubber gloves
brush

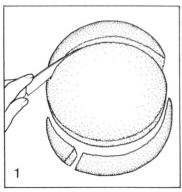

Cut two sides off cake to make it oval, then cut about 2.5cm (1in) off two leftover strips. These will become claws (fig 1).

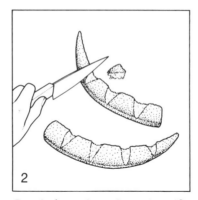

Cut indentations in strips (fig 2).

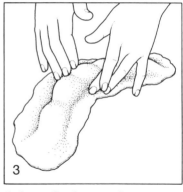

Colour fondant, using orange and red and wearing rubber gloves. Roll out small piece of fondant and cover jammed claw, pressing and moulding icing into shape (fig 3).

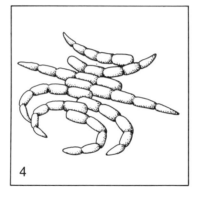

Cover other claw. Model eight small claws out of fondant (fig 4).

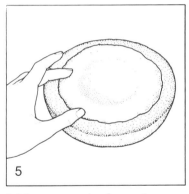

5

6

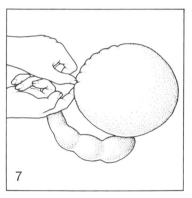

7

Stick a mound of marzipan to top of crab body to round it (fig 5).

Cover sides of body. Cover top, leaving a lip extending over the edge (fig 6).

Crimp edge of shell with fingers (fig 7).

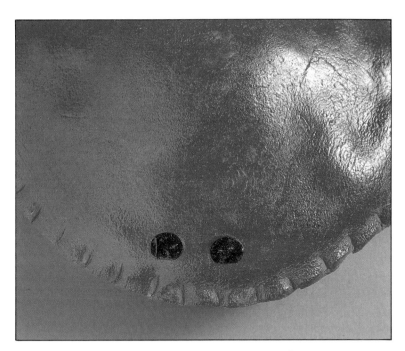

Cut two little liquorice eyes and stick in position. Put crab on board and stick claws to body with a little fondant or jam. With sponge dab on yellow and brown colouring to give speckled effect. Brush him with a little glycerine water to make him shiny if you like.

PLATE OF SPAGHETTI

PLATE OF SPAGHETTI

THIS VERY SILLY CAKE IS easy and quick to do, and as pasta is so popular with children nowadays I think it would make a good birthday cake. I've moulded the plate out of icing, but you could just as well put it on a real plate if you haven't time. The spaghetti looks fine without sauce (*al burro?*) but I've added 'Neapolitan sauce and parmesan' to finish it off. I found a strawberry pie filling which looks pretty good, but you might find an even more tomatoey-looking sweet sauce; let me know if you do.

EASY.
START TWO DAYS BEFORE IF YOU WANT AN ICING PLATE,
OR SAME DAY IF YOU USE A REAL ONE.

INGREDIENTS

For plate
225g (½lb) gelatine icing
icing sugar for rolling
green food colour

For spaghetti
1 18cm (7in) sandwich sponge
225g (½lb) butter icing
225g (½lb) royal icing
yellow or brown food colours
strawberry fruit filling
ground almonds

EQUIPMENT
real plate for moulding or using
piping bag and No 4 plain nozzle
paint brush
cake board

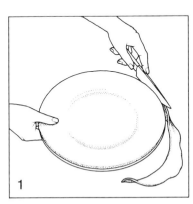

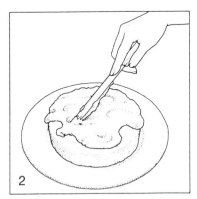

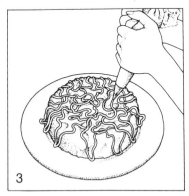

1 Dust the plate well with corn-flour. Roll out the gelatine paste and cover the plate, trimming neatly round the edge with a sharp knife (fig 1).

2 Let the plate dry well, for about 12 hours, then remove and paint a pattern round the edge. Put the cake onto the plate (icing or real) and spread with the butter icing, coloured cream (fig 2).

3 Colour the royal icing cream, then pipe all over the cake until it looks like spaghetti (fig 3).

Add fruity 'tomato sauce' and ground almonds 'parmesan' if desired.

THE SWIMMER

THE SWIMMER

T HE IMAGE OF THE British holidaymaker is never very glamorous but I'm quite fond of this happy chap, although I am rather worried about his colour now we know what terrible damage the sun does to our pale, sensitive skins . . .

MEDIUM DIFFICULTY.
START TWO DAYS BEFORE.

INGREDIENTS
1 SPHERICAL CAKE APPROX 12CM (5IN) DIAMETER
(I COOKED MINE IN A CHRISTMAS PUDDING TIN, BUT A
PUDDING BASIN CAKE WOULD DO JUST AS WELL).
1 mini roll
icing sugar for rolling
jam for sticking
350g (¾lb) marzipan
675g (1½lb) fondant
pink, blue and red food colours

EQUIPMENT
cake board
paint brush
non-stick baking parchment

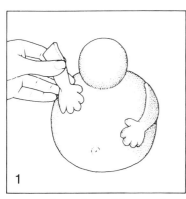

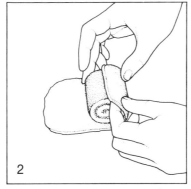

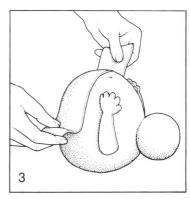

Cover the cake with marzipan to give it support. Let dry a little. Colour three-quarters fondant pink. Cover the cake with pink fondant then roll a head and stick it on with a little water or jam. Mark a 'tummy button'. Roll and cut two arms and stick them on (fig 1).

Cut two feet and set aside. Let all dry on baking parchment for 12 hours or so. Cut the mini roll in half and roll each half in marzipan (fig 2). Cover with pink fondant and let dry for 12 hours or so.

Cut a strip of white fondant and stick to lower half of body (fig 3).

THE SWIMMER

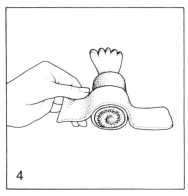

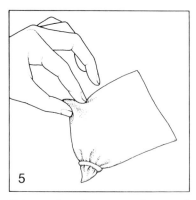

Stick feet to bottom of legs. Cover top of legs with white fondant (fig 4).

Paint red stripes onto legs and body. Stick body onto legs. Roll and cut a square 'handkerchief'. Pinch the corners, then add tiny strips to look like knots (fig 5).

Stick handkerchief onto head. Add a little fondant nose. Paint nose, cheeks and mouth red and eyes blue.

AUGUST *LEO*

LEO

THIS CAKE WAS INSPIRED by a beautiful one made by Greg Robinson and Max Schofield in their lovely book. It's a very useful technique to build up shapes in this way with marzipan *under* the icing.

MEDIUM DIFFICULTY.
START DAY BEFORE.

INGREDIENTS
1 30cm (12in) round shallow cake
450g (1lb) marzipan
900g (2lb) fondant
jam for sticking
icing sugar for rolling
450g (1lb) butter icing
brown, yellow, black and red food colours

EQUIPMENT
30cm (12in) cake board
paint brush

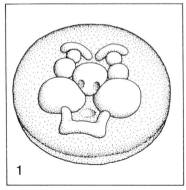

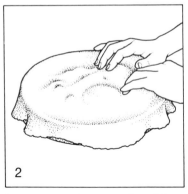

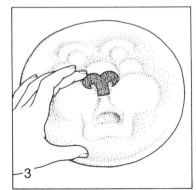

Model basic features out of the marzipan and stick to the cake with jam (fig 1).

Scoop out the mouth with a knife. Keeping back a small amount for teeth, eyes, nose and inside of mouth, colour most of the fondant, using a mixture of brown and yellow. Stick the cake to the board then jam it and cover with the rolled out fondant, pressing and moulding it round the features and into the mouth (don't worry if it breaks there) (fig 2).

Trim round the edge of the board. Cut a nose shape out of white fondant and stick it to the face with a little water (fig 3).

Build up features with more yellow fondant. Line the mouth with a little white fondant. Cover eyes with scraps of fondant. Paint the eyes, nose and inside of mouth then add fondant teeth. Colour the butter icing and spread it over the top of the head (fig 4).

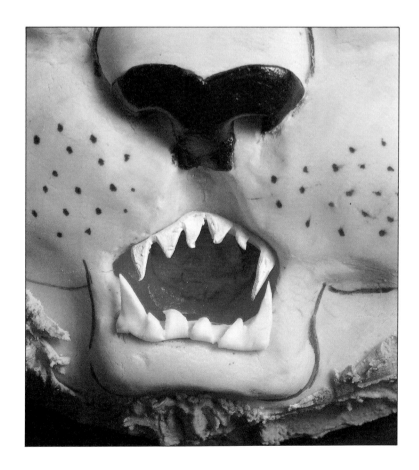

CROCODILE

CROCODILE

'How cheerfully he seems to grin
How neatly spreads his claws!'
as Alice would have put it. (In fact I think this is probably more like an alligator than a crocodile.)
It is much easier to make than it looks and it's one of my favourites.

MEDIUM DIFFICULTY.
START DAY BEFORE.

INGREDIENTS
1 bought swiss roll
2 mini rolls
1 doughnut
675g (1½lb) fondant
jam for sticking
icing sugar for rolling
green, brown and black food colours
tiny amount of royal icing or broken nuts for teeth
glycerine water for glazing

EQUIPMENT
cake board
mosaic cutter
piping bag and No 1 nozzle
paint brush
rubber gloves

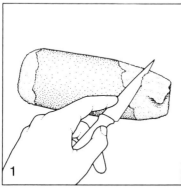

Shape the ends of the swiss roll so they slope off (fig 1).

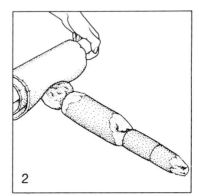

Stick the doughnut to one end of the roll with jam, then stick the two mini rolls the other end. Shape the end mini roll to slope off. Wearing rubber gloves, colour all the fondant browny-green and roll out nearly half of it. Jam the cake and drape the icing right over it (fig 2).

CROCODILE

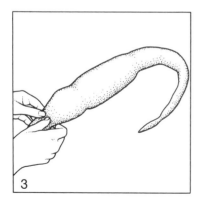

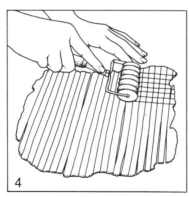

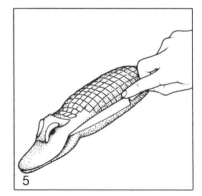

Trim the sides of the crocodile but leave the surplus at each end – join any spare icing with the half you kept back. Shape a long tail from the surplus icing. Mould the icing over the doughnut head and shape a snout from the surplus (fig 3).

Roll out half the remaining icing and cut squares, using a rolling mosaic cutter or any other suitable device (or a knife if necessary) (fig 4).

Damp the cake and stick the squares all over the back and head. Mark the features with a knife (fig 5).

Mould legs from remaining icing. Stick to crocodile with water. Add little balls of icing for eyes. Paint them black. Pipe tiny teeth with royal icing (or use broken nuts). Glaze him with glycerine water.

ROSE BOWL

ROSE BOWL

THIS WOULD BE A PERFECT Mother's Day cake if you don't think she'd appreciate the Sink (page 37). Roses are very easy to make out of icing, but look really impressive. You could of course make lots of different flowers, or even use fresh ones if you made holes in the cake first with a skewer.

EASY IF YOU USE FRESH FLOWERS, MEDIUM IF YOU MODEL THEM.
START FEW DAYS AHEAD TO GIVE YOU TIME TO MAKE THEM.

INGREDIENTS
3pt pudding basin cake (exact size doesn't matter)
450g (1lb) fondant to cover cake
jam for sticking
icing sugar for rolling
1.3kg (3lb) fondant to make roses
225g (½lb) fondant to make leaves
yellow, orange and green food colours
small amount of royal icing (or watered down fondant) for sticking

EQUIPMENT
cake board
non-stick baking parchment
cocktail sticks
kitchen paper

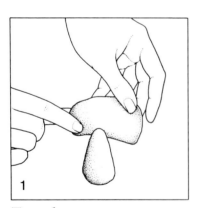

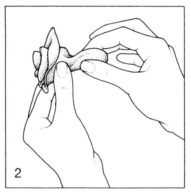

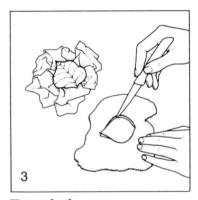

To make roses
Colour half the fondant yellow. Keep it in a plastic bag while you are working. Pull off a small piece and make a cone shape and put it on a surface. Pull off another small piece and press it with fingers well dusted with icing sugar until it is roughly petal shape. Damp the lower edge with water and stick it to the cone (fig 1).

Continue to build up petals in this way – about 5 or 6 for a full rose, two or three for a bud. Pick up the rose and twist off all the surplus icing from the bottom to make a nice neat shape (fig 2). Colour the rest of the fondant a more orangey yellow and make more roses. I made about 24 full roses and 12 buds altogether. Leave them all to dry on baking parchment.

To make leaves
Colour the fondant dark green. Roll it out and cut out rose leaf shapes. Mark the veins with a knife and leave them on crumpled kitchen paper so they dry in curly shapes (fig 3).

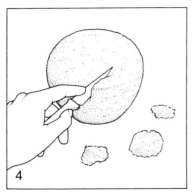

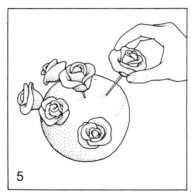

To make bowl
Trim the top of the cake so that it is rounded (fig 4). Cover it with white fondant.

Gently push a cocktail stick into each rose and push into the cake (fig 5). Stick the leaves between the roses with a little royal icing (or fondant mixed with water). Please remember to remove the cocktail sticks before eating.

VIRGO

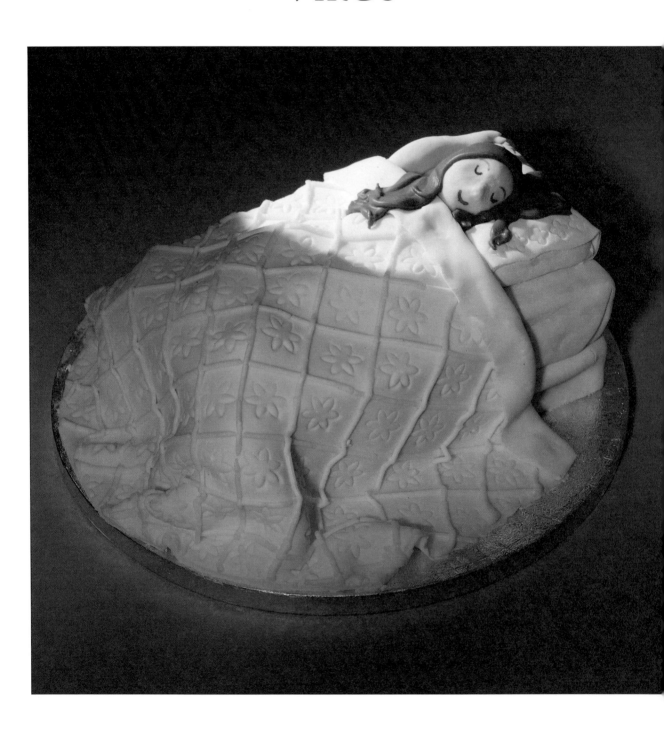

SEPTEMBER *VIRGO*

This isn't an easy star sign to portray without causing undue giggles. I decided a beautiful young girl alone in her bed sleeping peacefully between virginal white sheets would sum it up quite well (of course what you and I don't know is that there is probably a handsome icing prince hiding under the bed . . .)

MEDIUM DIFFICULTY.
START TWO DAYS AHEAD.

INGREDIENTS
cake baked in a tray about 22cm × 33cm (9in × 13in)
jam for sticking
icing sugar for rolling
900g (2lb) fondant
225g (½lb) white marzipan
225g (½lb) royal icing
pink and brown food colours

EQUIPMENT
small and tiny flower cutters to make patterns
piping bag with No 2 and flat ribbon nozzles
non-stick baking parchment
1 30cm (12in) cake board

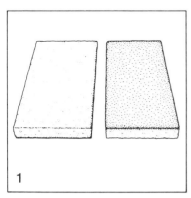

1

Trim cake and cut in half lengthways (fig 1).

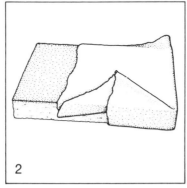

2

Jam top of one piece of cake. Roll out about a quarter of the fondant and cover most of the cake. Ice the other piece of cake in exactly the same way but make 'envelope corners' as shown (fig 2).

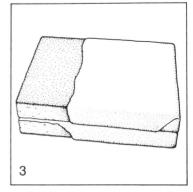

3

Stick the two pieces together with jam (fig 3). Stick to the cake board with a little icing.

VIRGO

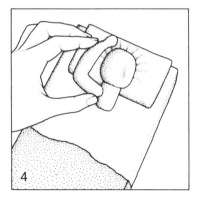

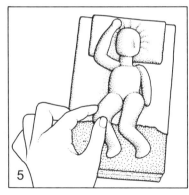

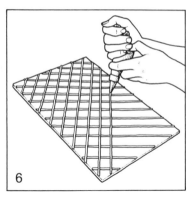

Mould a little pillow out of marzipan. Cover it with fondant then mark a few creases with a knife and some patterns with the tiny flower cutter. Stick it onto the bed with a little water. Colour a small amount of fondant pale pink, then model a head and arm and stick them to the pillow (fig 4).

Roughly model the rest of the body from marzipan and stick it to the bed (fig 5).

Keeping back a small amount to make the top sheet, roll out the remainder of the fondant on a piece of baking parchment. Measure over the bed with a piece of string, allowing extra for 'drape' then cut the fondant to size. Working quickly, pipe lattice pattern with the royal icing and No 2 nozzle (fig 6). Again working quickly so the lattice doesn't dry out and break, add patterns with flower cutter.

Drape the cover quickly over the bed, making folds with your fingers and trimming edges as necessary. Touch up any broken lattice work. Roll out the remaining fondant and cut a narrow strip. Tuck over top of 'bedspread'. Colour small amount of royal icing brown and pipe hair using the ribbon nozzle. Paint eyes and mouth.

SCHOOLBOY

SCHOOLBOY

M Y SEVEN-YEAR-OLD SON calmly announced one day last year that 'we have to take a special cake to school tomorrow for the end of term party'. Help! I rushed round the corner to my local shop and bought a jam sandwich and a doughnut and made him this schoolboy cake – it was a great hit with his classmates. I've adapted it here for going back to school, but it would make a lovely birthday cake or for any school occasion.

EASY.
START DAY BEFORE.

INGREDIENTS
1 20cm (8in) round cake
1 doughnut
675g (1½lb) fondant
225g (½lb) royal icing
icing sugar for rolling
jam for sticking
green and red food colours

EQUIPMENT
cake board
piping bag with Nos 1 and 3 nozzles

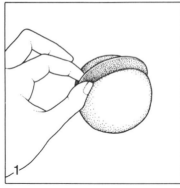

Level the top of the cake or use the underneath. Jam the cake and use about two-thirds of the fondant to drape over. Colour a small amount of fondant pink then cover the doughnut with it. Colour small amount of fondant green, and cover the top of his head. Stick the head onto the cake. Cut out a little peak from green fondant and stick upright onto cap, holding with the fingers until it is dry enough to stand up (fig 1).

Cut a tie from green fondant and stick below head. Cut two white triangular pieces to make the collar. Cut out tiny badge shape and stick to cap. Roll a little round nose from pink fondant and attach to face. Pipe eyes and mouth with No 3 nozzle and white stripes on tie with No 1. Colour remaining royal icing red, then pipe stripes onto tie, badge details and writing on cake (fig 2).

SING A SONG OF SIXPENCE

SING A SONG OF SIXPENCE

Nursery rhymes are a very good source of material for cake ideas; in spite of children becoming so much more sophisticated nowadays they still seem to love the old favourites. The pie crust looks very realistic made out of the marzipan, and if you don't want to model the blackbirds then you could always fill the gap with cherries or pieces of cooked apple to look like a fruit pie – if you used a bought cake you could make it in about 10 minutes!

EASY.
START BLACKBIRDS DAY BEFORE.

INGREDIENTS
*cake cooked in a 20cm (8in) round tin with
sloping sides like a pie dish
(or an ordinary sandwich tin would do)
jam for sticking
icing sugar for rolling
675g (1½lb) white marzipan
black, brown and yellow food colours
silver balls*

EQUIPMENT
*non-stick baking parchment
brush
rubber gloves*

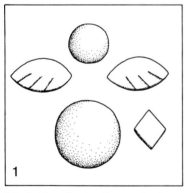

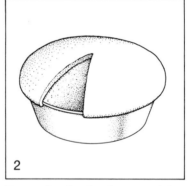

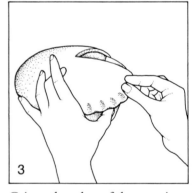

Model heads, bodies and wings of blackbirds out of marzipan and cut little diamond shapes for beaks (fig 1).

Press the beaks into position with the back of a knife so they bend in the middle. Stick the heads and wings onto the bodies with a little water or jam. Let the birds dry on baking parchment. Leave the cake in the tin and spread the top with jam. Roll out the remaining marzipan and drape it over the top. Trim round the edge then cut out a slice (fig 2).

Crimp the edge of the marzipan (fig 3).

Add three 'pastry' leaves. Brush the top of the pie with a little watered down brown colour to look cooked. Paint the birds black and their beaks yellow. Push in silver balls for eyes. Place the birds in the pie opening – yes I know there aren't 24, but the others are hiding under the crust . . .

LIBRA

I HAD WONDERFUL IDEAS about doing a beautiful lady holding some scales, or even making suspended weighing plates with little icing chains holding them up, but in the end went for simplicity. It might be fun to make bathroom scales instead – especially if the Libran concerned is a weight-watcher!

MEDIUM DIFFICULTY.
START TWO DAYS BEFORE TO LET WEIGHTS DRY.

INGREDIENTS
shallow cake cooked in a
25cm×30cm (10in×12in) roasting tin
900g (2lb) fondant
350g (¾lb) gelatine icing
jam for sticking
icing sugar for rolling
black and gold food colours

EQUIPMENT
chess pieces for moulding
round cutters
non-stick baking parchment
paint brush
Libra sign to copy

Roll out the gelatine icing and mould a small plate just as for spaghetti (page 69). I used a doll's plate as the template. Cut out a square plate (I used a china box to cut round). Mould the weights over chess pieces (see page 94) and cut the round ones with cutters. Let dry then add handles to the upright ones. Jam the cake and cover sides then top with fondant. Stick two

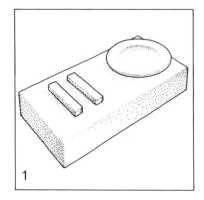

strips of icing onto one side of the top to raise up the plate (fig 1).

Stick the plates onto the cake. Paint the Libra sign on the side. Paint the weights gold (remember you shouldn't eat these) and place on the cake.

HALLOWE'EN

HALLOWE'EN

I'T'S GREAT FUN TO HAVE a party at this time of year, and the spookier you make everything the better. Any sort of witch, spider or ghost cake will do, but as my boys are very keen on Ghostbusters at the moment I designed this cake with one of their favourite characters on the top. If you don't feel up to modelling it out of icing, why not buy one and put it on the top as a special present?

MEDIUM DIFFICULTY.
START TWO DAYS AHEAD TO ALLOW MODEL TO DRY.

INGREDIENTS
1 25cm (10in) hexagonal cake
900g (2lb) fondant
225g (½lb) gelatine icing
jam for sticking
icing sugar for rolling
black, green and red food colours
125g (¼lb) royal icing

EQUIPMENT
toy to copy
hexagonal cake board
non-stick baking parchment
piping bag with No 2 nozzle
rubber gloves

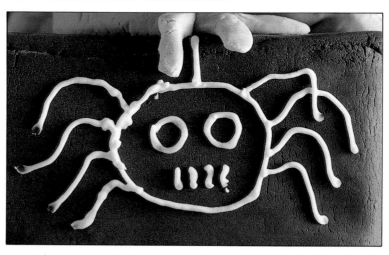

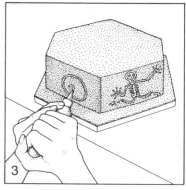

1 Colour the gelatine icing bright green, keeping a tiny amount back for the eyes, tongue and teeth. Model a ghost or similar, using a toy to copy. Leave it to dry on baking parchment, propping the mouth and arms with kitchen paper as necessary (fig 1).

2 Colour the fondant black (do remember to wear rubber gloves!) Jam the cake and cover the sides first (fig 2).

Turn the cake upside down onto rolled out icing to cover the top, or use the cake tin as a template. Roll the leftover fondant thinly and cover the board. Stick the cake to the board.

3 Pipe spooky characters round the sides with the royal icing (fig 3).

Add teeth, eyes and a tongue to the ghost. Let dry a little. Paint the features and stick him to the top of the cake.

DRAUGHTS OR CHESS

DRAUGHTS OR CHESS

I F YOU MAKE THE DRAUGHTS this cake is very easy and quick, but the chess pieces do take time. It would look wonderful as a centrepiece if you made the entire set, but as you can see I gave up after only four. Presumably the game is all over as there is only one king on the board . . .

EASY WITH DRAUGHTS, QUITE TRICKY WITH CHESS PIECES.
START DAY BEFORE WITH DRAUGHTS, TWO DAYS WITH CHESS.

INGREDIENTS
30cm (12in) square cake, about 5cm (2in) deep
jam for sticking
900g (2lb) fondant icing
icing sugar for rolling
black food colouring pen
brown and black food colours

For set of draughts
450g (1lb) fondant
brown and black food colours

For each chess piece
50g (2oz) gelatine icing
small quantity of royal icing
black food colour

EQUIPMENT
36cm (14in) square cake board
ruler
paintbrush

round cutters or suitable objects to
cut and mark draughts
chess pieces for moulding
piping bag with No 2 nozzle

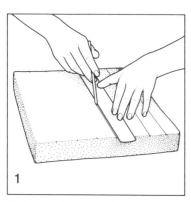

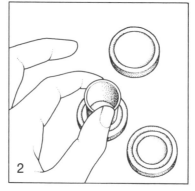

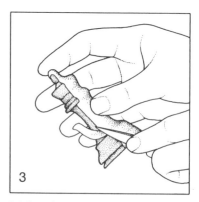

Colour fondant brown. Jam cake, roll out fondant and cover sides and then top to make neat corners. Rule 7 lines across each way with icing pen to make 64 squares (fig 1). Paint alternate squares with black food colour.

To make draughts: colour half the fondant with a tiny bit of brown to make a cream colour. Roll out and cut 12 cream draughts and 12 white. Mark surface of draughts with rings (fig 2). Paint white draughts black.

Make chess pieces in same way as teapot spout (p. 54) (fig 3). Stick together. Paint some black. Put onto the chess board (in an interesting chess move if possible?)

NOVEMBER *SCORPIO*

SCORPIO

SCORPIONS ARE FASCINATING creatures – I copied this one from a natural history book, and it's one of the highly poisonous types. The sandy effect of the sugar works very well, and could be useful for doing all sorts of desert scenes.

MEDIUM DIFFICULTY.
START DAY BEFORE.

INGREDIENTS
2 20cm (8in) round sandwich tin cakes
(coffee would be lovely?)
225g (½lb) coffee butter icing
75g (3oz) light golden soft brown sugar
600g (1¼lb) fondant
black and brown food colours
2 silver balls
jam for sticking
icing sugar for rolling
glycerine water for glazing

EQUIPMENT
rubber gloves
thick florists' wire
cake board
brush

Sandwich cakes together with two-thirds of the butter icing. Jam side of cake. Colour about two-thirds of the fondant brown. Measure height of cake and circumference with a piece of string, then roll out fondant and cut to fit. Stick to side. Spread remaining butter icing on top then sprinkle the brown sugar onto it. Colour the remaining fondant black, wearing rubber gloves. Model the body of the scorpion first and mark his back with a knife. Press two silver balls in for his eyes. Put him on the cake.

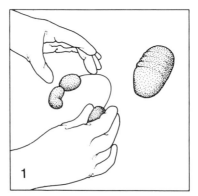

Curve a piece of florists' wire and stick it in position for his tail. Model little pieces of fondant and thread them onto the wire (fig 1).

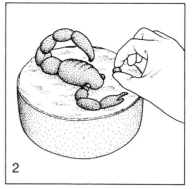

Model arms and claws and place them on the cake, sticking them to each other with a little water (fig 2).

Glaze the scorpion with glycerine water.

BONFIRE NIGHT

EVEN IF YOU'RE NOT celebrating November 5th itself (and I think fireworks are much better watched at public displays than at home) this would be a lovely November birthday cake. If you find the Guy difficult you could always just make the bonfire (*very* easy) and put a doll on top. I found the wonderful chocolate twigs in a local delicatessen, but if you can't find them it would look almost as good with just Matchmakers.

EASY.
START DAY BEFORE (TO ALLOW GUY TO DRY).

INGREDIENTS
1 cake cooked in a 3 pt pudding basin
(chocolate would be lovely)
350g (¾lb) chocolate butter icing
1 box Matchmakers
1 box chocolate twigs
(or another box of Matchmakers)
350g (¾lb) fondant
food colours

EQUIPMENT
3 cocktail sticks
cake board

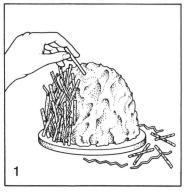

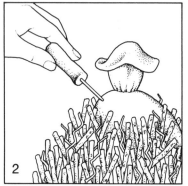

Put cake on board and spread liberally with chocolate butter icing (you could also split the cake in two and sandwich with icing if you like). Press the Matchmakers and twigs into the icing (fig 1).

Colour the fondant suitably to make the Guy and his clothes – it doesn't matter how rough he looks as he's only meant to be made of old bits of material. Make the body first and push it into the top of the bonfire. Model the head and attach it with a cocktail stick to the body, then make the arms and use sticks to support them too (fig 2). Do remember to remove the cocktail sticks before eating.

BRIDE

BRIDE

A LOVELY CAKE FOR A little girl's birthday – or I suppose you could use it for a wedding, but it would mean modelling a groom out of fondant which might end up looking a bit strange . . . The doll used in the cake could be an extra present for the birthday girl, or you could use a favourite doll and clean her up a bit. Do make sure the doll's legs are removable and replaceable if you want to keep her – the only doll I could get at short notice when making my cake had to have her legs surgically removed with the kitchen scissors!

MEDIUM DIFFICULT, DEPENDING ON LACE METHOD.
START TWO DAYS AHEAD.

INGREDIENTS
1 cake cooked in a 3½pt pudding basin
jam for sticking
icing sugar for rolling
900g (2lb) fondant
450g (1lb) royal icing
floral icing bouquet

EQUIPMENT
1 suitable size doll
cake board
small piece of net
small piece of florists' wire, or fuse wire
piping bag and No 2 nozzle
non-stick baking parchment

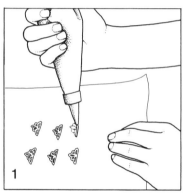

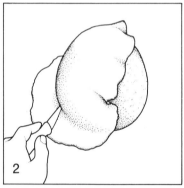

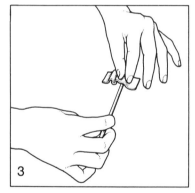

Put about half the royal icing into the piping bag. Draw a lace shape onto a piece of paper and slide it under the baking parchment. Using this as a guide, pipe a lace shape. Move the drawn lace from place to place under the parchment until you have piped about 80 shapes (that allows a few for breakage). Pipe a few flowers freehand for the front of the dress. Leave for a couple of days to dry (fig 1). If you like you can pipe the trimmings directly onto the cake which is much easier but not quite so delicate-looking.

Using 225g (½lb) fondant cover about half of the cake, sticking with jam as usual, and trim round the bottom (fig 2).

Remove the legs from the doll and push into the top of the cake. Cut pieces of fondant and stick to doll with water to make her bodice. Roll out two more small strips and pleat them with fingers and the end of a brush or something similar to make her sleeves (fig 3).

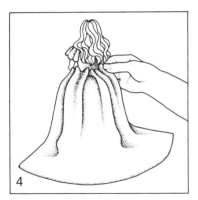

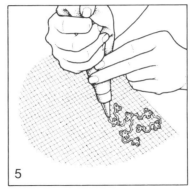

Stick the sleeves in position. Roll out remainder of fondant and drape over back of jammed cake to make train. Pleat and fold it as you go, to look like material. Trim the edge as necessary. Make a little peplum in the same way as you did the sleeves and stick to her waist (fig 4).

Tidy the doll's hair (I found it best to chop mine off completely). Cut the net to the right size for her veil, then spread it over baking parchment and pipe a floral design all over it and a pattern round the edge. Work quickly, as it cracks if you let it get dry (fig 5).

Put a little icing on the doll's hair for sticking, then drape the veil over. Pipe a 'head-dress' at the front. Stick the lace all round the edge of the skirt and train and the flowers onto the front. I cheated and asked a friend Mrs Tilbrook to make me a bouquet, as she can make the most amazing tiny flowers. If you aren't lucky enough to have such a friend, then either take a two-year icing course (!!) or buy some ready made from a specialist cake shop (or you might find some tiny fresh flowers that would do).

SAGITTARIUS

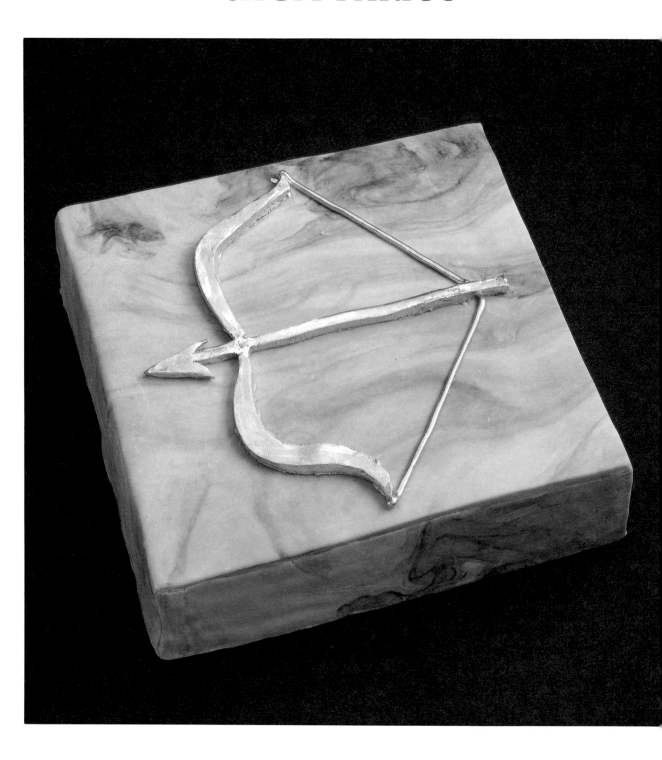

DECEMBER *SAGITTARIUS*

THIS SIMPLE TECHNIQUE of cutting a shape out of icing and putting it on top of a cake can be very useful and effective. I got the idea for the marbling from seeing the beautiful patterns that emerged whenever I was kneading colour into fondant – you could do it with pink, blue or green for all sorts of different ideas.

EASY.
START SAME DAY.

INGREDIENTS
23cm (9in) square cake
900g (2lb) fondant
jam for sticking
icing sugar for rolling
125g (¼lb) royal icing
black and silver food colours

EQUIPMENT
cake board
paper and pencil
paint brush
non-stick baking parchment
piping bag with No 2 nozzle
rubber gloves

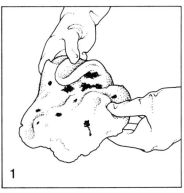

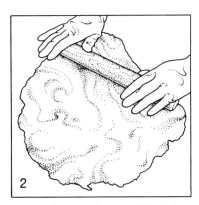

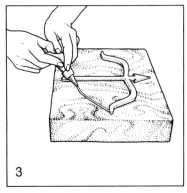

Draw a bow and arrow minus its string on the paper, cut it out then use as a template to cut the shape out of rolled out fondant. Let dry a little on baking parchment. With the end of the paint brush, dot black colouring onto the remaining fondant. Mix it in very slightly, wearing rubber gloves (fig 1).

Dust the surface with icing sugar and roll out the fondant until marbling patterns appear (fig 2). (Check the underneath, as sometimes the patterns are even better there.)

Jam the cake and cover with fondant, doing sides first and then top, to achieve a crisp block shape. Stick the bow and arrow to the top of the cake with a little icing, then pipe the string (fig 3). When dry paint silver.

FATHER CHRISTMAS

FATHER CHRISTMAS

CHRISTMAS IS SUCH A busy time that it's good to have a simple idea for the cake, and either this jolly Santa or the Snowman looks much more fun on the festive table than the usual rugged snowscene with plaster figures. You could always make a sack for Father Christmas and fill it with tiny presents or sweets to make it even more exciting.

EASY.
START DAY BEFORE.

INGREDIENTS
cake cooked in a 3½ pt pudding basin
2 doughnuts
jam for sticking
icing sugar for rolling
675g (1½lb) fondant
225g (½lb) royal icing
red and blue food colours
licorice whirl

EQUIPMENT
cake board
piping bag with No 2 nozzle and small shell nozzle
rubber gloves

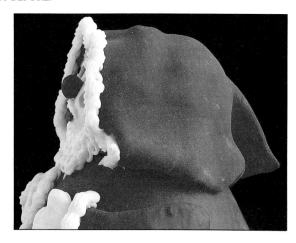

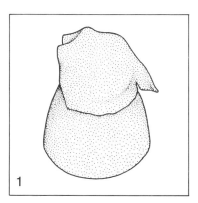

Make a head with two dough-nuts in exactly the same way as for Snowman (page 109), except you only need to cover the front of the head with icing. Wearing rubber gloves, colour nearly all the remaining fondant

red, saving a small white bit for his nose and gloves. Cover the cake entirely with the red. Stick the head to the body with water or jam. Roll out a wide strip of red fondant and drape it over the head to make the hood. Pinch the hood together at the back (fig 1).

Add a little round nose to the face, then pipe eyes, mouth, hair, beard and moustache with the royal icing and No 2 nozzle (fig 2). Cut two red arms and stick to body.

Cut out two white gloves and stick to body. Pipe trimming on coat and hood using shell

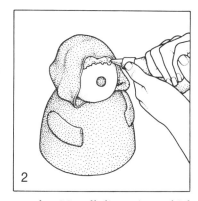

nozzle. Unroll liquorice whirl and cut to the right length for his belt, then stick to the body with a little royal icing. Paint eyes blue, cheeks, nose and mouth red.

CABBAGE

CABBAGE

T HIS WAS INSPIRED BY ONE of Kaffe Fassett's beautiful tapestry designs. It would be a lovely centrepiece for a harvest festival or a keen gardener's birthday.

MEDIUM DIFFICULT.
START THREE DAYS AHEAD.

INGREDIENTS
*1 spherical cake. Mine is about
15cm (6in) diameter
and I cooked it in a Christmas
pudding tin,
but you could shape a pudding
basin cake
900g (2lb) gelatine icing
jam for sticking
icing sugar for rolling
675g (1½lb) fondant
green and brown food colouring
225g (½lb) royal icing
350g (¾lb) marzipan*

EQUIPMENT
*1 Savoy cabbage
cake board
shallow bowl
paint brush
kitchen paper
plastic bag*

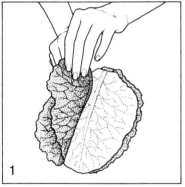

Take about two-thirds of the gelatine icing, keeping remainder safely in a plastic bag. Roll out a quarter of the larger amount about 5mm (¼in) thick. Remove a large outer leaf from the cabbage, place on the work surface and dust with icing sugar. Drape the rolled icing over the leaf, then press a second, similarly sized leaf on top. Trim round the edge and gently push together, to mark both surfaces of the icing. Remove leaves (fig 1).

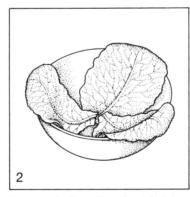

Dust a shallow bowl with icing sugar, then drape the icing leaves into the bowl so that the tops fold over the edge. Make four or five leaves in this way, putting any leftover icing with the piece you've already saved. Leave to dry (fig 2).

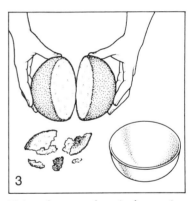

Trim the two hemispheres (or shape your pudding basin cake) and join together with jam (fig 3).

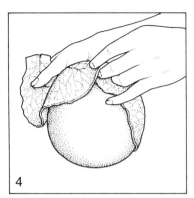

4

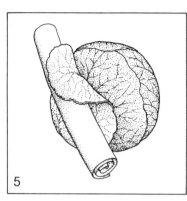

5

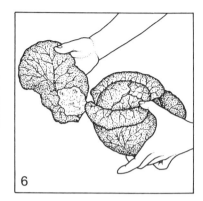

6

Jam the sphere and cover with marzipan (this is not essential, but it makes the cake easier to work with). Make three fondant leaves, using the method above, but only marking the underneath surfaces, and stick them with jam overlapping onto the cake (fig 4). Let dry a little.

Mix a pale green wash and brush it over the iced cake. Roll out the remaining gelatine icing and make three more leaves. Damp the leaves with water and stick them to the cake, curling back the top edges. Prop them up with rolled kitchen paper while they dry (fig 5).

When dry, mix a darker green wash and brush over the curled leaves. Stick the other dried gelatine leaves onto the cake with royal icing (fig 6.).

Let the royal icing dry. Paint the outer leaves dark green, then, using the real cabbage as a guide, add darker tones and brown.

SNOWMAN

SNOWMAN

THIS IS MADE IN THE SAME way as Father Christmas and is very easy to do. I have made the arms from the wonderful chocolate twigs that I found for the bonfire, but Matchmakers or even twiglets would do just as well.

EASY WITHOUT THE TOP HAT, START TWO DAYS AHEAD IF YOU WANT TO MAKE THAT.

INGREDIENTS	EQUIPMENT
cake cooked in a 3½pt pudding basin	*cake board*
2 doughnuts	*cocktail stick*
675g (1½lb) fondant	*object to mould hat round*
jam for sticking	*rubber gloves*
icing sugar for rolling	*non-stick baking parchment*
2 chocolate twigs, or Matchmakers	*skewer*
black, green and orange food colours	*plastic bag*

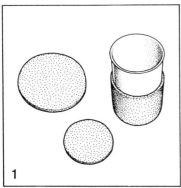

1

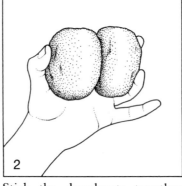

2

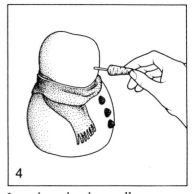

4

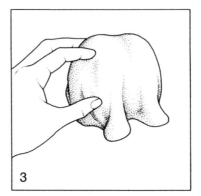

3

Colour 125g (¼lb) fondant black, wearing rubber gloves. Find an object of suitable size and cut a circle of black fondant from it to be the top of the hat. Cut a circle for the brim a bit larger (it needn't have a hole in the middle). Dust the object well with icing sugar and wrap a strip of fondant round it to be the side of the hat. (Keep scraps of black fondant to make eyes and buttons later.) Leave all to dry on baking parchment (fig 1).

Stick the doughnuts together with a little jam (fig 2).

Roll out about one-third of the remaining fondant. Jam the doughnuts then wrap the icing around them (fig 3).

Jam the cake then roll out most of remaining fondant. Drape it over cake. Stick head to body with jam or by wetting the icing. Colour a little fondant green, cut out and fringe a scarf. Stick it round his neck. Make eyes and buttons from the black fondant and stick on. Colour a scrap of fondant orange, model a carrot and push in place on a cocktail stick (fig 4).

Carefully remove side of hat. Stick the pieces together with a little watered down black fondant. Stick hat to head. Make holes in his sides with skewer and push in arms. Don't forget to remove the cocktail stick safely before it is eaten.

INDEX